# DATE DUE

| | | | |
|---|---|---|---|
| | | | |
| | | | |
| | | | |
| | | | |
| | | | |
| | | | |
| | | | |
| | | | |
| | | | |
| | | | |
| | | | |
| | | | |
| | | | |
| | | | |
| | | | |
| | | | |
| | | | |
| | | | |
| | | | |
| | | | |
| | | | |

Demco, Inc. 38-293

# THE AUTOMOBILE
# AND THE
# ENVIRONMENT

# EARTH • AT • RISK

Acid Rain

Alternative Sources of Energy

Animal Welfare

The Automobile and the Environment

Clean Air

Clean Water

Degradation of the Land

Economics and the Environment

Environmental Action Groups

Environmental Disasters

The Environment and the Law

Extinction

The Fragile Earth

Global Warming

The Living Ocean

Nuclear Energy • Nuclear Waste

Overpopulation

The Ozone Layer

The Rainforest

Recycling

Solar Energy

Toxic Materials

What You Can Do for the Environment

Wilderness Preservation

EARTH • AT • RISK

# THE AUTOMOBILE AND THE ENVIRONMENT

by Maxine Rock

Introduction by
Russell E. Train
Chairman of
the Board of Directors,
World Wildlife Fund and
the Conservation Foundation

CHELSEA HOUSE PUBLISHERS

new york   philadelphia

CHELSEA HOUSE PUBLISHERS
EDITOR-IN-CHIEF: Richard S. Papale
MANAGING EDITOR: Karyn Gullen Browne
COPY CHIEF: Philip Koslow
PICTURE EDITOR: Adrian G. Allen
ART DIRECTOR: Maria Epes
ASSISTANT ART DIRECTOR: Howard Brotman
MANUFACTURING DIRECTOR: Gerald Levine
SYSTEMS MANAGER: Lindsey Ottman
PRODUCTION COORDINATOR: Marie Claire Cebrián

EARTH AT RISK
Senior Editor: Jake Goldberg

Staff for *The Automobile and the Environment*
COPY EDITOR: Ian Wilker
EDITORIAL ASSISTANT: Danielle Janusz
PICTURE RESEARCHER: Villette Harris
SERIES DESIGNER: Maria Epes
SENIOR DESIGNER: Marjorie Zaum
COVER ART: Paul Biniasz
COVER ILLUSTRATION: Debora Smith

First printing
1  3  5  7  9  8  6  4  2

Library of Congress Cataloging-in Publication Data
Rock, Maxine A.
  The automobile and the environment/by Maxine Rock;
  introduction by Russell E. Train
     p. cm.—(Earth at risk)
  Includes bibliographical references and index.
  Summary: Discusses the automobile's role in polluting the
environment and ways of decreasing the damage.
   ISBN 0-7910-1592-0
        0-7910-1617-X (pbk.)
   1. Automobiles—Motors—Exhaust gas—Environmental
aspects—Juvenile literature. 2. Transportation,
Automotive—Environmental aspects—Juvenile literature. 3.
Carbon monoxide—Environmental aspects—Juvenile literature.
[1. Automobiles—Motors—Exhaust gas—Environmental aspects.
2. Air—Pollution. 3. Pollution.] I. Title. II. Series.      91-37271
TD886.5.R64 1992                                              CIP
363.73'87—dc20                                                AC

# CONTENTS

# INTRODUCTION

Russell E. Train

Administrator, Environmental Protection Agency, 1973 to 1977; Chairman of the Board of Directors, World Wildlife Fund and The Conservation Foundation

There is a growing realization that human activities increasingly are threatening the health of the natural systems that make life possible on this planet. Humankind has the power to alter nature fundamentally, perhaps irreversibly.

This stark reality was dramatized in January 1989 when *Time* magazine named Earth the "Planet of the Year." In the same year, the Exxon *Valdez* disaster sparked public concern over the effects of human activity on vulnerable ecosystems when a thick blanket of crude oil coated the shores and wildlife of Prince William Sound in Alaska. And, no doubt, the 20th anniversary celebration of Earth Day in April 1990 renewed broad public interest in environmental issues still further. It is no accident then that many people are calling the years between 1990 and 2000 the "Decade of the Environment."

And this is not merely a case of media hype, for the 1990s will truly be a time when the people of the planet Earth learn the meaning of the phrase "everything is connected to everything else" in the natural and man-made systems that sustain our lives. This will be a period when more people will understand that burning a tree in Amazonia adversely affects the global atmosphere just as much as the exhaust from the cars that fill our streets and expressways.

Central to our understanding of environmental issues is the need to recognize the complexity of the problems we face and the relationships between environmental and other needs in our society. Global warming provides an instructive example. Controlling emissions of carbon dioxide, the principal greenhouse gas, will involve efforts to reduce the use of fossil fuels to generate electricity. Such a reduction will include energy conservation and the promotion of alternative energy sources, such as nuclear and solar power.

The automobile contributes significantly to the problem. We have the choice of switching to more energy efficient autos and, in the longer run, of choosing alternative automotive power systems and relying more on mass transit. This will require different patterns of land use and development, patterns that are less transportation and energy intensive.

In agriculture, rice paddies and cattle are major sources of greenhouse gases. Recent experiments suggest that universally used nitrogen fertilizers may inhibit the ability of natural soil organisms to take up methane, thus contributing tremendously to the atmospheric loading of that gas—one of the major culprits in the global warming scenario.

As one explores the various parameters of today's pressing environmental challenges, it is possible to identify some areas where we have made some progress. We have taken important steps to control gross pollution over the past two decades. What I find particularly encouraging is the growing environmental consciousness and activism by today's youth. In many communities across the country, young people are working together to take their environmental awareness out of the classroom and apply it to everyday problems. Successful recycling and tree-planting projects have been launched as a result of these budding environmentalists who have committed themselves to a cleaner environment. Citizen action, activated by youthful enthusiasm, was largely responsible for the fast-food industry's switch from rainforest to domestic beef, for pledges from important companies in the tuna industry to use fishing techniques that would not harm dolphins, and for the recent announcement by the McDonald's Corporation to phase out polystyrene "clam shell" hamburger containers.

Despite these successes, much remains to be done if we are to make ours a truly healthy environment. Even a short list of persistent issues includes problems such as acid rain, ground-level ozone and smog, and airborne toxins; groundwater protection and nonpoint sources of pollution, such as runoff from farms and city streets; wetlands protection; hazardous waste dumps; and solid waste disposal, waste minimization, and recycling.

Similarly, there is an unfinished agenda in the natural resources area: effective implementation of newly adopted management plans for national forests; strengthening the wildlife refuge system; national park management, including addressing the growing pressure of development on lands surrounding the parks; implementation of the Endangered Species Act; wildlife trade problems, such as that involving elephant ivory; and ensuring adequate sustained funding for these efforts at all levels of government. All of these issues are before us today; most will continue in one form or another through the year 2000.

Each of these challenges to environmental quality and our health requires a response that recognizes the complex nature of the problem. Narrowly conceived solutions will not achieve lasting results. Often it seems that when we grab hold of one part of the environmental balloon, an unsightly and threatening bulge appears somewhere else.

The higher environmental issues arise on the national agenda, the more important it is that we are armed with the best possible knowledge of the economic costs of undertaking particular environmental programs and the costs associated with not undertaking them. Our society is not blessed with unlimited resources, and tough choices are going to have to be made. These should be informed choices.

All too often, environmental objectives are seen as at cross-purposes with other considerations vital to our society. Thus, environmental protection is often viewed as being in conflict with economic growth, with energy needs, with agricultural productions, and so on. The time has come when environmental considerations must be fully integrated into every nation's priorities.

One area that merits full legislative attention is energy efficiency. The United States is one of the least energy efficient of all the industrialized nations. Japan, for example, uses far less energy per unit of gross national product than the United States does. Of course, a country as large as the United States requires large amounts of energy for transportation. However, there is still a substantial amount of excess energy used, and this excess constitutes waste. More fuel efficient autos and home heating systems would save millions of barrels of oil, or their equivalent, each year. And air pollutants, including greenhouse gases, could be significantly reduced by increased efficiency in industry.

I suspect that the environmental problem that comes closest to home for most of us is the problem of what to do with trash. All over the world, communities are wrestling with the problem of waste disposal. Landfill sites are rapidly filling to capacity. No one wants a trash and garbage dump near home. As William Ruckelshaus, former EPA administrator and now in the waste management business, puts it, "Everyone wants you to pick up the garbage and no one wants you to put it down!"

At the present time, solid waste programs emphasize the regulation of disposal, setting standards for landfills, and so forth. In the decade ahead, we must shift our emphasis from regulating waste disposal to an overall reduction in its volume. We must look at the entire waste stream, including product design and packaging. We must avoid creating waste in the first place. To the greatest extent possible, we should then recycle any waste that is produced. I believe that, while most of us enjoy our comfortable way of life and have no desire to change things, we also know in our hearts that our "disposable society" has allowed us to become pretty soft.

Land use is another domestic issue that might well attract legislative attention by the year 2000. All across the United States, communities are grappling with the problem of growth. All too often, growth imposes high costs on the environment—the pollution of aquifers; the destruction of wetlands; the crowding of shorelines; the loss of wildlife habitat; and the loss of those special places, such as a historic structure or area, that give a community a sense of identity. It is worth noting that growth is not only the product of economic development but of population movement. By the year 2010, for example, experts predict that 75% of all Americans will live within 50 miles of a coast.

It is important to keep in mind that we are all made vulnerable by environmental problems that cross international borders. Of course, the most critical global conservation problems are the destruction of tropical forests and the consequent loss of their biological capital. Some scientists have calculated extinction rates as high as 11 species per hour. All agree that the loss of species has never been greater than at the present time; not even the disappearance of the dinosaurs can compare to today's rate of extinction.

In addition to species extinctions, the loss of tropical forests may represent as much as 20% of the total carbon dioxide loadings to the atmosphere. Clearly, any international approach to the problem of global warming must include major efforts to stop the destruction of forests and to manage those that remain on a renewable basis. Debt for nature swaps, which the World Wildlife Fund has pioneered in Costa Rica, Ecuador, Madagascar, and the Philippines, provide a useful mechanism for promoting such conservation objectives.

Global environmental issues inevitably will become the principal focus in international relations. But the single overriding issue facing the world community today is how to achieve a sustainable balance between growing human populations and the earth's natural systems. If you travel as frequently as I do in the developing countries of Latin America, Africa, and Asia, it is hard to escape the reality that expanding human populations are seriously weakening the earth's resource base. Rampant deforestation, eroding soils, spreading deserts, loss of biological diversity, the destruction of fisheries, and polluted and degraded urban environments threaten to spread environmental impoverishment, particularly in the tropics, where human population growth is greatest.

It is important to recognize that environmental degradation and human poverty are closely linked. Impoverished people desperate for land on which to grow crops or graze cattle are destroying forests and overgrazing even more marginal land. These people become trapped in a vicious downward spiral. They have little choice but to continue to overexploit the weakened resources available to them. Continued abuse of these lands only diminishes their productivity. Throughout the developing world, alarming amounts of land rendered useless by over-grazing and poor agricultural practices have become virtual wastelands, yet human numbers continue to multiply in these areas.

From Bangladesh to Haiti, we are confronted with an increasing number of ecological basket cases. In the Philippines, a traditional focus of U.S. interest, environmental devastation is widespread as deforestation, soil erosion, and the destruction of coral reefs and fisheries combine with the highest population growth rate in Southeast Asia.

Controlling human population growth is the key factor in the environmental equation. World population is expected to at least double to about 11 billion before leveling off. Most of this growth will occur in the poorest nations of the developing world. I would hope that the United States will once again become a strong advocate of international efforts to promote family planning. Bringing human populations into a sustainable balance with their natural resource base must be a vital objective of U.S. foreign policy.

Foreign economic assistance, the program of the Agency for International Development (AID), can become a potentially powerful tool for arresting environmental deterioration in developing countries. People who profess to care about global environmental problems— the loss of biological diversity, the destruction of tropical forests, the greenhouse effect, the impoverishment of the marine environment, and so on—should be strong supporters of foreign aid planning and the principles of sustainable development urged by the World Commission on Environment and Development, the "Brundtland Commission."

If sustainability is to be the underlying element of overseas assistance programs, so too must it be a guiding principle in people's practices at home. Too often we think of sustainable development only in terms of the resources of other countries. We have much that we can and should be doing to promote long-term sustainability in our own resource management. The conflict over our own rainforests, the old growth forests of the Pacific Northwest, illustrates this point.

The decade ahead will be a time of great activity on the environmental front, both globally and domestically. I sincerely believe we will be tested as we have been only in times of war and during the Great Depression. We must set goals for the year 2000 that will challenge both the American people and the world community.

Despite the complexities ahead, I remain an optimist. I am confident that if we collectively commit ourselves to a clean, healthy environment we can surpass the achievements of the 1980s and meet the serious challenges that face us in the coming decades. I hope that today's students will recognize their significant role in and responsibility for bringing about change and will rise to the occasion to improve the quality of our global environment.

A sheet music cover from the 1920s for a tune made popular by singer Al Jolson reveals that even then the automobile was a great source of frustration.

chapter 1

# BIRTH OF THE AUTOMOBILE

The United States has more cars—and more car owners—than has any nation on earth. But the automobile was actually born in France in 1770 when an army captain, Nicolas Cugnot, invented a small steam tractor designed to haul cannon. An odd three-wheeled conveyance with a huge steam drum attached to the front, it was nonetheless the first road vehicle that could travel by itself, even if it did have to stop every ten minutes to build up steam.

Almost 40 years later, an English inventor named Richard Trevithick converted the steam tractor to a four-wheeled wagon designed to transport passengers. This rough ancestor of the automobile was more popular at first as a plaything than as a serious form of transportation, but it caught on quickly. By the 1830s, "steam carriages" were terrorizing pedestrians in England with loud belching noises, blasts of dirty smoke, and an occasional sizzling lump of coal, which flew from its engine and often set fire to nearby crops and wooden bridges. Citizens called for laws to control these frightening machines, and in 1865 Parliament obliged. It passed the Locomotives Act, which set rigid speed limits on steam carriages and forced drivers to hire signalmen to walk ahead and warn of the vehicle's approach.

It was thus obvious from the start that the automobile would be an environmental hazard as well as a revolutionary method of transportation. Almost as soon as it was invented, the auto spurred laws trying to control the noise, air, and visual pollution it created.

By the late 19th century, steam automobiles were firing the imagination of American inventors. The Stanley twins, Francis and Freelan, became famous for their Stanley Steamer, and Ransom Eli Olds even sold steam cars overseas (the first export went to Bombay, India, in 1893). But steam cars were hard to start, slow moving, and frightening because they required an open fire and hot steam for power. Looking for an alternative, an Iowa inventor named William Morrison came up with an auto that ran on electricity. He built his first electric car in 1890, and it immediately became more popular than steam cars because it was quiet and did not emit intolerable fumes. Batteries on the electric car, however, had to be recharged every 50 miles or so, and it could not travel faster than 20 miles per hour.

In 1860 the French inventor Jean Joseph Etienne Lenoir developed the first gas-burning auto. In 1876 a traveling sales- man named Nikolaus August Otto, improving on Lenoir's design, built the first modern, four-cycle internal combustion engine, and within a few years he was selling thousands of them to new automaking firms. In Germany, Gottlieb Daimler, who built gasoline-powered motorcycles, and Karl Benz, who put gasoline engines in three-wheeled autos, made further improvements. American inventors saw the possibilities for widespread manufacture of gas autos and experimented with many different

*One of the earliest gasoline-powered, reciprocating engines, developed by Gottlieb Daimler in 1883.*

forms until Charles and Frank Duryea premiered their elegant canopied gas auto in 1894. The car was a big hit, and the Duryea brothers opened the first American company for the manufacture of gas autos just one year later.

## MASS PRODUCTION

The best-known names in American auto history—Henry Ford, Ransom Eli Olds, William Durant, and others—are known not for inventing these machines but for successfully manufacturing and selling them. Europeans may have dreamed up the auto, but the American genius lay in making it available to ordinary people. In 1901, the same year that huge new oil fields were discovered in eastern Texas, managers at the Olds Motor Works in Detroit, Michigan, created the first auto *assembly line*. These two events opened the way for mass production of the automobile.

By 1914, assembly line methods were sophisticated enough to have finished cars rolling through the factory doors at the rate of about one every hour and a half. Every new time-saving device or method meant that the cost of the auto could be further reduced. In 1916, Henry Ford was able to sell his Model T for less than $400, a lower price than any of his competitors could offer. His reward was that between 1908 and 1927, over half the autos sold in the United States were Fords. During World War I, the same mass production techniques that worked for the auto were used to churn out military trucks and tanks, and by the time the war ended in 1919 the auto industry was the third most

*The first motorcar manufactured by Henry Ford in a small workshop in Detroit in 1896. The car weighed about 500 pounds and was supported by bicycle tires. Its 2-cylinder engine propelled it at 10 miles per hour.*

important business in the United States. It ranked right behind meat packing and iron and steel. During the 1920s, William Durant's General Motors (GM) merged with Buick, Cadillac, Oldsmobile, and several other makes of cars and became the United States's largest auto manufacturing firm. The electric starter, which did away with the backbreaking chore of cranking an engine by hand, was a General Motors innovation and further spurred public acceptance of private automobiles.

By the 1930s auto production in the United States was dominated by three giants: General Motors, Ford, and Chrysler. Cars became more graceful and—with the addition of an enclosed cab to protect riders from wind and rain—much more comfortable. Radios and heaters were installed, and so was shatterproof glass. Although the production of private autos nearly stopped in 1941 when the United States entered World War II, citizens were already addicted to having their own cars. When the war ended in 1945, people were delighted with further improvements in the private car such as curved windshields, automatic transmissions, stylish upholstery, and air-conditioning. Although European, Russian, Italian, and eventually Japanese manufacturers became strong automakers, the United States remains the world leader in producing, importing, and using automobiles.

## HOW THE MODERN AUTO WORKS

Though there are many different models and types, most modern gasoline-driven automobiles work the same way. When an auto's ignition switch is turned on, electric power flows from a battery to a small starter motor that starts the auto's engine. The starter motor spins a crankshaft that forces pistons to rapidly move up and down within their cylinders. The driver, by pressing his or her foot down on the accelerator, feeds a mixture of gas and air to the cylinders. The spark plugs, also activated by the ignition switch, ignite the mixture of gas and air in the cylinders. When the mixture burns, the pistons pump rapidly. As the pistons pump faster and faster, and the crankshaft turns swiftly, power from the engine is carried to the drive shaft and to the rear wheels. The auto is propelled forward.

It is the fuel-burning process that creates air pollution, the most obvious, and perhaps most dangerous, part of the auto's impact on the natural environment. Exhaust from auto engines (and from buses, trains, and ships as well) contains pollutants such as *carbon monoxide* gas; hydrocarbons, which are mixtures of hydrogen and carbon; and *nitrogen oxides*, compounds of nitrogen and oxygen. Nitrogen oxides produce *ozone*, which reacts with hydrocarbons to create the hazy type of air pollution called smog. After clean air standards were set in the late 1960s and emission control devices were invented for automobiles, air pollution from American cars has steadily decreased. By the early 1990s, hydrocarbon emissions had been reduced by 80% since 1968, and carbon monoxide emissions had gone down about 68%. Air pollution continues to go up worldwide, however, because there are more cars on the road.

## THE GOVERNMENT STEPS IN

As the auto evolved, it became increasingly obvious that this machine was changing the American way of life, and not always for the better. Now highways wiped out communities and neighborhoods. Parking lots began to replace parks. Malls and motels, or "motor hotels," often caused the demise of attractive sidewalk shops and gracious hotels. Traffic accidents became common, and in the early 1970s autos began killing far more Americans at a far greater rate—57,000 per year—than did even the two world wars. Dangerous fumes from cars darkened and polluted the air, and auto junkyards littered the American landscape. By late 1969 the environmental effects of the automobile were so pronounced that the federal government had to step in and impose some controls.

Although the federal government had shown concern over air pollution and other hazards as early as 1955, the first law with any real power to handle the problem was not passed until 1969. In that year the National Environmental Policy Act (NEPA) was created, stating that it was now the duty of the U.S. government to "encourage productive and enjoyable harmony between man and his environment."

NEPA meant that federal planners had to take the environment into account any time major government actions would significantly affect the environment. For example, if government funds were to go into a major roadbuilding project, a statement would have to be prepared showing how the project would affect air quality, water quality, and soil erosion. In 1970 a companion act to NEPA was passed, called the Environmental Quality Improvement Act. This set up the Office of Environmental Quality to study environmental problems and assist federal agencies in evaluating them. These two acts gave the federal government the authority to withhold public money from projects that would cause major environmental damage.

After 1970, government researchers were encouraged to take a hard look at the way the automobile was affecting the environment. They did not like what they saw. Air quality in urban areas, where autos were clustered within limited spaces and people could not escape their fumes, was alarmingly toxic. Congress quickly passed the Clean Air Act of 1977, creating the Environmental Protection Agency (EPA). The EPA was given the authority to set ambient air quality standards. It also had the power to force auto manufacturers to reduce the amount of emissions from their automobiles. From then on, producing a "clean car" became a major concern for the designers and builders of American automobiles.

That concern was heightened in November 1990 with the passage of major revisions to the Clean Air Act, the first time since 1977 that tough air pollution legislation seriously challenged the auto industry. The act acknowledged the need for more environmental responsibility on the part of U.S. auto manufacturers, but industry regulations were fought every inch of the way by White House chief of staff John Sununu and budget director Richard Darmon. These men shared President George Bush's opinion that attempts to protect the environment might hamper economic growth. Instead, White House policy on air pollution and energy centered around opening the Arctic National Wildlife Refuge and other potentially oil-rich areas to oil drilling, rather than finding alternative fuels, and accepted air pollution for the most part as a regrettable but necessary price of doing business.

Congress passed the revised Clean Air Act over the Bush administration's objections. When the law's toughest strictures go into effect in 2020, they are expected to cost the nation about $35 billion a year. Daniel Weiss, director of the Sierra Club's environmental quality program, says what we will get for this hefty price tag is that in the future "our air will be significantly cleaner."

The new Clean Air Act deals with much more than auto-related pollution problems. But it recognizes that emissions from motor vehicles are responsible for many environmental problems and mandates that auto exhaust fumes will have to be further reduced. Eventually, cleaner-burning gasoline will have to be sold in cities such as Chicago, Los Angeles, New York, and Philadelphia. Auto manufacturers will have to come up with cars that operate on alternative fuels or go out of business.

## THE BOSTON PLAN

With new federal regulations for clean air came a turnaround in public thinking about how to transport large numbers of people, particularly in cities. Planners had always linked "transportation" with "highway," assuming that citizens would get around just fine in their private automobiles if they had enough of the necessary surface pavement on which to drive. Now, however, widespread concern over air pollution has made transportation planners think more in terms of mass transit. Mass

*As late as the 1940s, in rural areas gasoline was sold mainly at the local general store.*

transit systems are less polluting than are automobiles, require less pavement, and move more people at less expense. Perhaps the first city to loudly declare that it wanted no more roads in urban areas was Boston. The city moved so fast—and so intelligently—to curtail road building and reduce air pollution that it stands out as a model of clear thinking and decisive action on this issue.

In February 1970, soon after the federal government first brought attention to the dangers of air pollution with its new laws, Mayor Francis Sargent of Boston ordered a moratorium on major highway construction in his city. Boston planners already had come up with the Boston Transportation Planning Review (BTPR), a blueprint for future highway construction and mass transit, but the Mayor wanted to curtail the highway plans and concentrate more on mass transit.

The Boston City Council agreed. For the next 18 months or so planners and citizens worked together to come up with nonpolluting transportation alternatives. There were open meetings on the subject, and people voiced their opinions in a friendly atmosphere. The result was a balanced transportation plan that included a mix of arterial roads, special purpose high-ways, and—perhaps most important—major improvements in Boston's mass transportation system. Any time federal, state, or local transportation planners get together now and voice a concern for the environment, they have the Boston plan as a model for solving the multiple pollution problems that go along with the automobile.

In the 1970s, spurred by Boston's leadership, other city officials clamored for—and got—federal help in transportation planning. Mass transit systems all over the country got a boost with the Urban Mass Transportation Assistance Act of 1970. This was followed by the Federal Aid Highway Act of 1970, which made it clear that highway planners had to take environmental costs, such as air pollution, into account every time they wanted to build a new road with federal funds. Even more laws regulating highway building were passed in 1973. By the mid-1970s, transportation studies and computer programs were helping urban planners reduce traffic flow and curb pollution. In 1977 amendments to the Clean Air Act increased local government's responsibility in curbing air pollution. Cities such as San Francisco responded by building elaborate light rail systems and encouraging commuters to use them instead of taking their cars to work.

With the administration of President Ronald Reagan in the 1980s there was once again a trend to decentralize decision making about air pollution and other transportation issues. In 1982 an executive order mandated that the states review their own transportation programs and that the federal government "accommodate" their decisions or "explain" why it would not. Since then transportation planning in the United States has been a constant tug-of-war, with environmentalists generally favoring stronger federal leadership, while others remain more concerned that local political bodies solve their own pollution problems.

Those problems are now having an important impact on everyday life for all American citizens. To help curb automobile-related pollution, Americans must face the challenge of using alternative transportation whenever possible, while auto designers struggle to create a less environmentally destructive machine.

*Heavy vehicle traffic moving through downtown Los Angeles creates a great deal of smog and gives the city one of the worst air quality ratings of any major American urban area.*

# H O W   A U T O S   P O L L U T E

Almost everything people do with their cars causes some form of pollution. Driving creates auto exhaust, which spews out chemicals and poisons the air. Oil spills and the dumping of auto-related refuse pollutes the water supply. Auto "graveyards" and tire dumps deface the landscape, and highway runoff is a major source of soil pollution. Making and using cars may be one of humankind's most polluting activities.

The fumes from automobiles, known as auto exhaust, contribute greatly to three of the biggest pollution problems in the world today: global warming, *acid rain*, and dirty air. Global warming is the result of a buildup of *carbon dioxide* ($CO_2$) and other gases in the atmosphere that entrap heat, leading to a long term warming of the earth's climate. The warming, which is predicted to push up global temperatures as much as 2 degrees to 9 degrees Fahrenheit by the middle of the next century, could threaten crops and produce mass famine, as well as melt polar ice caps and drown coastal areas under rising oceans.

A major ingredient in acid rain is nitrous oxide, created when gasoline is burned. Cars create at least one-third of all the nitrous oxide in the environment. Air pollution, or dirty air, appears mainly in the form of ground-level ozone, which forms when hydrocarbons and nitrous oxide from cars combine and are exposed to ultraviolet light from the sun. Nitrous oxide is also implicated in global warming, along with other pollutants that cars produce such as carbon dioxide from exhausts and *chlorofluorocarbons* from an auto's air conditioner.

There are about 135 million cars in America today, and it is no longer unusual for families to own several of them. The automobile has become almost a requirement for daily life in the United States. Although the United States has only about 4% of the world's population, its citizens own at least 48% of the world's cars.

Because autos are so important to the American economy, antipollution advocates here have a tough time translating their ideas into law. Supported by politicians who flinch at regulating big business, American automobile manufacturers fight fuel-efficiency standards so hard and so successfully that it is difficult to enact and monitor tough auto pollution legislation. The United States has the technology to produce cleaner cars, but to keep costs down the auto manufacturers' lobby exerts great pressure on federal legislators to discourage auto pollution control bills. The result is generally weak enforcement provisions of the air pollution control legislation that does exist. Some states have become so impatient with the federal government that they have passed clean air standards of their own: New York, New Jersey, and the six New England states recently joined to force automakers into meeting *emission standards* that are tougher than those imposed by federal law, and Vermont recently passed a bill that will outlaw air conditioners in automobiles unless a substitute is found for ozone-damaging chlorofluorocarbons.

A 1989 report by the World Health Organization and the United Nations Environment Program estimated that air pollution from automobiles has become a problem of serious proportions in at least half the cities of the world. *Lead* and carbon monoxide (both by-products of auto operation) are present in large cities worldwide in what the report calls "unacceptable" levels, threatening the health of children, the elderly, and fetuses. As the number of autos in the former Soviet Union and Eastern Europe grows, health hazards there from air pollution increase because there are virtually no controls on auto emissions in these areas of the world. Many Western European cities are suffering so badly from auto-generated air pollution that even a leading car manufacturer, BMW, has suggested that towns in Germany "need electric cars

*Automobile junkyards litter the American landscape. From such graveyards, oil, lead, and battery acids enter the ground and chlorofluorocarbons leak into the atmosphere.*

earlier than in California." BMW officials are concerned because clean-air legislation seems inevitable, and they have begun spending one-third of their $845 million annual research budget on alternative cars and cleaner-burning fuels.

Around the world, cities such as Athens, Budapest, and Mexico City now have to enforce emergency driving bans on hazy days so citizens do not choke to death on smog.

### AIR POLLUTION

Air pollution is made up of *particulates,* or tiny floating pieces of solid dirt, dust, soil, other natural materials, and chemical pollutants. Dirty air damages human lungs and causes health problems. It also soils fabrics, damages buildings and statues, reduces visibility, and, in the United States alone, costs about $20 billion a year in cleaning and replacement bills. The automobile is certainly not the only contributor to air pollution, but large numbers of autos seem to do most of the damage. About 20% of all $CO_2$ emissions in the United States come from cars.

The toxic mixture of chemicals in car exhausts is now recognized as a major hazard to human health. The American Lung Association says that air pollution from automobiles kills between 60,000 and 120,000 people in the United States each year and costs $93 billion in medical bills. Such pollution kills cells in the nose and causes burning in the eyes and throat. It damages the sensitive cilia (tiny hairs) that line the air-cleansing bronchiole tubes and may cause the lungs to age prematurely. It adds to the breathing problems of asthmatics and reduces lung function in healthy people. According to a 1990 study by cardiologists at the University of North Carolina, carbon monoxide from car exhausts may also cause potentially fatal heart rhythm disturbances in otherwise healthy people. Joggers who exercise close to a busy highway could be killed by inhaling too much carbon monoxide, researchers say. Because about 78 million Americans live in cities where carbon monoxide pollution is, according to the EPA, "unacceptable," cardiologists warn that the United States must tighten restrictions on auto emissions to protect the nation's health.

### GLOBAL WARMING

Carbon dioxide accounts for about half of the *greenhouse effect*, and autos create roughly 17% of the world's carbon dioxide. The earth's climate depends on a delicate balance between the energy gained from solar radiation and the energy lost by radiation from the earth's surface back into space. That balance is brought about by just the right amount of natural gases. If too much carbon dioxide is added to the air, too much heat energy is trapped in the atmosphere. This overheats the earth's surface. Scientists predict that this warming effect could cause drought, create deserts, melt glaciers and ice caps, change the patterns of tropical and monsoon rains, and flood many of the world's large population centers. Dr. Alexander Leaf, writing in the *New England Journal of Medicine* in 1991, said that physicians are worried about global warming because it could disrupt vegetation and agriculture in many parts of the world and cause millions to starve. Dr. Leaf warned that global warming "may create 50 million environmental refugees worldwide, more than triple the number of all refugees today."

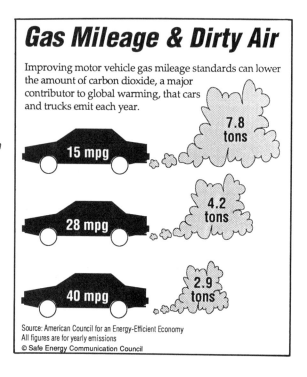

*A chart prepared by the Safe Energy Communication Council shows how cars that get better gas mileage also contribute less to the problem of global warming.*

**Gas Mileage & Dirty Air**

Improving motor vehicle gas mileage standards can lower the amount of carbon dioxide, a major contributor to global warming, that cars and trucks emit each year.

15 mpg — 7.8 tons

28 mpg — 4.2 tons

40 mpg — 2.9 tons

Source: American Council for an Energy-Efficient Economy
All figures are for yearly emissions
© Safe Energy Communication Council

## WATER POLLUTION

Motor oil, brake fluid, and transmission fluid dumped down the drain or into a sewer eventually winds up polluting the earth's soil and water. Antifreeze from automobiles is another common water pollutant. Large concentrations of antifreeze, poured into the nation's waterways, poison fish and wildlife and can also kill humans if they drink too much of it. Antifreeze that has been used in older cars may also contain hazardous concentrations of lead.

Vast numbers of automobiles also require vast supplies of oil, and oil has a tendency to be dumped into oceans as a result of accidental spills. Each year, such spills pour about 2.9 million barrels of oil into the sea. In New York City's harbor area alone, there is an average of one spill a day. The world environmental group Greenpeace has made the point that people prefer to blame oil companies when there is a spectacular spill like the Exxon *Valdez* disaster. To make people realize that overuse of the family auto was indirectly responsible for the tragedy of the Exxon *Valdez*, Greenpeace ran an advertisement showing a picture of the ship's captain with the caption, "It wasn't his driving that caused the Alaskan oil spill. It was yours."

## NOISE POLLUTION

Noise pollution from the honking horns, screeching tires, and grating gears of motor vehicles also erodes the quality of life in many cities worldwide. Health officials in large urban areas have set noise limits to curb noise pollution beyond levels at which it becomes difficult for people to hold conversations, read, listen to music, or even think. But those noise limits are regularly exceeded in New York City, Los Angeles, and other major urban areas. In downtown Cairo, Egypt, for example, noise levels are 10 times above the limit. This is a particularly difficult problem for people who have to live next to big highways. In Atlanta, Georgia, a concert pianist told city officials that when a big backyard highway, Interstate 75, was built within 500 feet of her backyard, she could no longer practice the piano or concentrate on reading music. Medical researchers have documented the effects of noise on human health and say that the roaring engines and blaring horns of automobiles cause high blood pressure, stomach upset, and even irregular heartbeat.

Every year, American drivers throw away 247 million auto tires. Nine million junked cars a year are added to auto graveyards. Old auto batteries leak sulfuric acid and lead into the soil as they disintegrate, and 64 million of them are tossed away yearly. Only a fraction of the billion tons of steel in these junked autos is ever recycled.

Scrap material from used autos can be successfully recycled. The United States did it during World War II when the careful use and reuse of materials helped the war effort. When the war ended, however, Americans developed a throwaway mentality. It was assumed that the nation was so big that citizens

*At Eastern Products in Malden, Maine, researchers are experimenting with new technologies that will allow the mixing and burning of used rubber tires with coal to produce energy.*

would never run out of places to throw their garbage, even garbage as big as an old automobile. It was also assumed that the country was so rich in natural resources that it was cheaper and more convenient to use new materials than to reuse the old.

Now, however, recycling is slowly coming back into vogue, partly because the United States has run out of space, partly because strategic resources are becoming scarce, and partly because people are beginning to be repelled by the look of a landscape filled with auto junkyards. In addition, the environmental savings of recycling can no longer be ignored. For example, if a steel mill uses recycled scrap metal instead of iron ore, it can reduce its water pollution by 76% and its mining wastes by 97%.

In addition to steel, many of the other materials that go into a car can also be recycled. Battery recycling is routine in Europe and Japan, and may be slowly catching on in the United States. Glass is 100% recyclable, even if it is broken. Broken glass, called cullet, is simply added to new molten glass in a furnace and can be reused indefinitely. Used oil is a valuable national resource, and many American communities are now starting curbside collection programs to recycle old oil. Used tires can be shredded and made into sheet rubber and other products. Recycling old autos and auto parts is an effective way to save money and conserve natural resources.

*Vail, Colorado, a winter resort town that has banned cars from its downtown streets and commercial areas.*

# H O W   T H E   A U T O
# S H A P E S   O U R   L I V E S

The private automobile has changed the landscape of the United States and restructured the daily life of its people. Before cars became the main mode of transportation for most families in this country, there were sharp geographic divisions between city and countryside. But with access to an auto, farm families could remain in close touch with urban areas and thus revolutionize their social and business lives. City people used cars to expand the boundaries of their recreational activities, and a new form of business arose devoted to the motoring vacationer, consisting of motels, roadside restaurants, service stations, quick-stop shopping marts, and other roadside commercial enterprises.

The auto demands roads, and roads are often expanded into highways. Much of the American landscape has been transformed by highways. In 1921, when autos were still owned mainly by the rich, the United States had 387,000 miles of surfaced roads. By 1940, when mass production had made cars available to the general public, there were 1,340,000 miles of roads. Today the number of miles of paved-over land is virtually uncountable, and among the most powerful political bodies in state and federal government are the highway and transportation departments.

The auto has also become a status symbol. Having an automobile is a ticket to fast, convenient, personalized travel, and the owner of a fine auto gains prestige because it indicates great personal wealth. Within families, finally gaining access to the automobile is an important ritual of growing up. The auto is also granted to youngsters as a reward or withheld as a form of punishment.

The auto is so much a part of American life that the country is known worldwide as a "nation on wheels." People routinely plan their daily schedules around the car, and having "wheels" affects the choice of neighborhood, job, and school. Automobiles are so central to daily life in the United States that even during the Great Depression of the 1930s, when auto sales collapsed, auto ownership did not. People just kept their old cars running longer. The car had already become second only to the house as a mark of the "good life" in the United States.

But this good life comes with a high price. Older cities that were built as places where people walked to business and social events are now packed with automobiles, and newer communities are so auto-oriented that many of them do not even have sidewalks. Traffic congestion is a familiar and frustrating fact of daily life in most urban areas. As transportation expert Wilfred Owen, writing about how the car has clogged modern life, laments, "The automobile is an irresistible force that may become an immovable object, and in the process destroy the city."

The automobile has led to the creation of modern suburbia, shopping malls, drive-in banks and theaters, motels, superhighways, and gas stations. Autos also influence how new

*Americans have become so car-dependent that they now demand drive-in services, such as this drive-in bank, that completely eliminate the need for getting out and walking.*

housing units are constructed; in the United States they are often placed on widely-spaced lots far from shopping centers and other workplaces, because builders assume homeowners will have a car. Auto congestion has dictated working hours in some areas and erased entire communities to make way for paved parking lots. Without people fully realizing it, the auto has become one of the prime determinants of our national way of life. It is a machine that now dominates many major life-style decisions.

HOUSING

Early communities prospered near waterways, where ships were used to transport goods and passengers, so that ports and river towns became great cities. In the 1830s, railroads revolutionized world transportation and people who settled near large clusters of train tracks (such as Atlanta, Georgia, which was first known as Terminus because the railroad terminated there) were soon living in the centers of commerce. But the method of transportation with the greatest impact on housing—especially in the United States—has been the private automobile. In the 1950s the emergence of the affordable, mass-produced automobile coincided with the surging popularity of suburban single-tract family housing. From then on, many middle-class communities were designed on the assumption that residents would be almost totally dependent on the automobile.

Oddly enough, although automobile ownership has virtually erased pedal power as a serious form of transportation for American adults, it was the humble bicycle that literally paved the way for the dominance of the auto. It was not until the 1930s that bicycles became sleek and sturdy enough to provide reliable transportation in cities and surrounding towns, and ordinary working people depended on their bikes to get them to work and school. Bicyclists demanded smooth, safe roadways because it was dirty and difficult to ride on unpaved trails. It was this demand that led to the first serious efforts at highway improvement in the United States, just before the auto became affordable for the masses. Inventors who were developing pneumatic rubber tires for bicycles quickly adapted their creations for the automobile.

The automobile has separated social classes in many parts of the United States by confining many of the poor who do not own automobiles to congested inner cities and allowing the middle and upper classes (who own one or more cars) to commute to the city by day and flee from it at night. In the process, says urban planner Donald Appleyard, everyone suffers. Inner cities are clogged and ugly, and suburban dwellers have lost all sense of neighborhood and community because they travel alone, locked in their cars. In his book *Livable Streets*, Appleyard says that the overuse of cars and the proliferation of parking lots close to homes disrupt urban life and degrade housing choices. He points out that when people depend on autos too much, they gradually change traffic signals, pathways, and open spaces to favor drivers, not pedestrians. Instead of making streets places where children play and adults converse or shop, says Appleyard, cars turn the streets into inhospitable and dangerous roads. A quiet, safe, clean, and pleasant neighborhood is not possible where the auto is allowed to remain unchecked, he declares.

It does not have to be this way. Pleasant streets where people live in harmony with the environment are possible, and they do not have to exclude cars. Car use can be controlled, not eliminated, in such areas. One example is Barnsbury, a com-

*A typical American suburb, with garages and driveways but no sidewalks. This type of community and the whole life-style based on it would not have been possible without the automobile.*

munity of Georgian brick houses north of London, England. To restore Barnsbury to its pre-auto quality of life, urban planners asked residents how the automobile affected them. Overwhelmingly, the people said they were most bothered by traffic jams, air pollution, noise, and not being able to walk safely on the streets. Using these complaints as a basis for change, planners figured out how to make Barnsbury more livable by curbing auto use in the area. Traffic was limited to essential vehicles, and "rat-runners," people who zoomed through the neighborhood in souped-up cars, were ticketed. Commuter parking garages replaced on-street parking. A pedestrian network was planned so people could stroll to shops and to the homes of neighbors. A recent report on Barnsbury says that as a result of controls on auto use, the area has become a highly desirable residential neighborhood where children can play safely and

*This Central Valley, California, "shopping center," photographed in 1940, was a precursor of the modern shopping mall.*

"considerations of the environment dominate over the use of vehicles."

It is easy to find places like Barnsbury in Europe, where narrow streets, many urban parks, and a walk-around mentality invite residents and city planners to choose a way of life that is not dominated by the automobile. But finding examples of non-auto communities in the United States is much harder.

Still, the auto is recognized by many American planners as a potential enemy in urban communities, and more and more city dwellers in the United States are demanding a quieter and cleaner way of life. They get it, so far, mainly on vacation, in places such as Vail and Beaver Creek, two resort communities located close to one another in the mountains of Colorado. Vail is a 25-year-old planned community nestled at the base of several ski mountains. It was modeled after an alpine village, with the same steepled buildings, narrow walkways, and charming courtyards as one might see in a mountainside town in Switzerland. No cars are allowed on the main streets of Vail. People may drive to the village but must park in underground lots and walk to the shops, restaurants, chalets, and ski facilities within the town center. The idea has been a huge success, and Vail is consistently rated a top resort by people from all over the world. They enjoy not only the skiing but also the calmness and relaxation that goes with not having to dodge autos or put up with traffic and auto-related noise.

Beaver Creek, about eight miles from Vail, is a newer community which has adopted Vail's no-auto stance. This cluster of homes, shops, hotels, and ski facilities, also located at the base of a mountain, was constructed in such a way that auto transportation within its core is impossible. The main part of Beaver

Creek is a pedestrian walkway accessible by ramps, stairways, and walking and biking trails. There is one road leading to the village, but drivers must leave their cars in an underground lot to enter the walkways or must return to the bottom of the roadway and use a large parking lot there. A walking and biking trail winds up the mountain, further inviting visitors and residents to abandon their cars and enjoy the view on foot. Visitors to Beaver Creek consistently applaud the village's emphasis on pedestrian comfort. People who have a hard time getting around on foot are served by free minibuses which circulate frequently around the fringes of the village.

## TRANSPORTATION PLANNING

People seem happy to leave their cars and get around on foot or by bicycle when they're on vacation, but can the idea work in busy everyday communities? Only if rapid transit, in the form of buses, light rail commuter trains or subways make it easy and convenient to leave the auto at home. Unless an area is actually built—as Vail and Beaver Creek were—with the no-auto concept in mind from the very start, it takes expert transportation planning and political determination to convert habitual auto users into people who are content with another way to get around.

One successful residential community that has been built with walkers and bicycle riders in mind is Peachtree City, Georgia. All of its 40,000 residents live in homes, apartments, and condominiums nestled close to a 45-mile network of auto-free paths. The paths lead to shops, schools, offices, medical facilities, libraries, playgrounds, parks, and neighbor's homes. They skirt two 250-acre lakes and travel through tunnels under main streets.

*As far back as 1941, traffic jams plagued Sunday drivers on their way to the beaches of Long Island in New York.*

Every resident in Peachtree City can walk, ride a bicycle, or use an electric golf cart to travel anywhere in the community.

The federal government has traditionally dismissed success stories like Peachtree City and encouraged planners and builders to construct communities with the auto in mind. In most cases, when state and local governments look for ways to solve a transportation problem, about 90% of the federal money they are offered is earmarked for highway construction, and almost no financial aid is given for non-auto pathways and rapid transit. State governments are often dominated by rural legislators, who push for roads because they equate auto traffic with an economic shot in the arm. In addition, there are many small local political bodies which exert pressure on transportation planners to consider their special needs. In America there is a strong tradition of individual protest against any form of large-scale government planning, and zoning laws are often bent to suit the complaints or needs of a neighborhood or even a developer. In Europe it is easier to plan for mass transit and for the phase-out of the auto because in these nations there is a strong tradition of centralized government control.

Still, there has been much recent progress in planning for mass transit and curbing the use of the automobile in America. Boston forbids much on-street parking in its city center, encouraging people to walk or take the train. Philadelphia has been interested in curbing auto use since 1959, when it contracted with the Pennsylvania Railroad to provide better commuter service. The federal government now regularly awards grants for the building of rail lines to communities that can demonstrate a well-planned strategy for replacing car use with mass transit.

### TRAFFIC ACCIDENTS

It is impossible to talk about how the auto has affected human life without discussing traffic accidents. Death by automobile is now rated by the Atlanta-based Centers for Disease Control as the third-leading cause of death among Americans,

*Not the least of the problems created by the automobile is the inability of many drivers to control it. Traffic accidents kill thousands of Americans every year.*

right after cancer and heart disease. Traffic accidents have killed more people in this country than have all its wars combined, and each year one-quarter of a million people worldwide die beneath the wheels of an automobile. Millions of yearly injuries in every nation are attributed to auto-related accidents.

The government and automakers constantly look for ways to make autos safer, yet the sheer number of cars in use every day pushes accident statistics higher and higher. In America, the National Highway Traffic Safety Administration sets safety standards for autos, which now include safety-oriented technologies such as seat belts, shatterproof windows, impact-absorbing bumpers, and collapsible steering columns. Still, an estimated 14,000 lives are lost yearly in this nation because people simply fail to buckle their seat belts. Because so many people ignore safety precautions while driving, many new cars come equipped with passive restraint systems, such as seat belts that automatically wrap around passengers or air bags that inflate at the time of a collision to cushion a car's occupants from a crash. The combination of more sophisticated safety devices in cars, plus less use of cars in favor of walking, bicycles, and mass transit, should bring down the numbers of people hurt and killed by automobiles.

The energy crisis came home in the 1970s. Cars formed long lines at this Los Angeles gas station in 1979, when rationing was introduced based upon odd- and even-numberd license plates.

chapter 4

# THE ENERGY CRISIS

The fuels burned in automobiles are the refined fossilized remains of plants and animals that lived centuries ago. As scientist Carl Sagan has noted, by using fossil fuels "we subsist on the dead bodies of our distant relatives."

The energy crises the world has experienced in modern times, so far, are not the result of running out of these fuel supplies, although they are a finite resource and will eventually be exhausted. Recent crises have been caused because fossil-fuel reserves are located mostly below Middle Eastern nations with unstable governments that can quickly turn hostile to the United States and other oil-dependent nations and cut off fuel supplies. When President Saddam Hussein ordered Iraqi troops into neighboring Kuwait in August 1990, he was attempting to take control of nearly 20% of the world's proven oil reserves. The result was Operation Desert Storm, a military assault by the United States, France, England, and other nations that joined in a coalition to free Kuwait and its oil supplies.

In initiating Operation Desert Storm, President George Bush noted that he was sending troops into battle on foreign sands "to protect our way of life." Opponents of the war took this to mean that President Bush was equating the American way of life with cheap, easily accessible oil supplies. It is true that the United States is painfully dependent on foreign oil; more than half of the oil used in this country is purchased from other nations, and well over half of the annual U.S. trade deficit comes from oil imports costing $50 billion yearly. It is clear that oil is used mainly to keep cars running: 43% of all the *petroleum* used goes into the tanks of American automobiles and light trucks.

A crisis also exists because of the realization that fuel supplies, although abundant, cannot last forever. The United States was oil-rich just several decades ago, but with the proliferation of the automobile the fuel beneath the continental United States has been sucked nearly dry. Exploring for oil in the ocean and in national parks and wilderness areas threatens to destroy fragile ecosystems and is strongly opposed by conservation groups. Even if the Bush administration is successful in opening the entire coast of Alaska and the Arctic National Wildlife Refuge to oil companies (to name just one possible area of exploration), experts estimate that the oil gained would only keep the United States's cars on the road for one more year. Thus the United States now must buy the oil it needs from other nations, which will also eventually run dry. Only 5% of the world's total remaining oil reserves lie under U.S. soil.

FUEL CONSERVATION

The political instability plaguing the oil-producing Persian Gulf nations underscores the need for fuel conservation in the Western world. Of all the industrialized nations, the United States is the most wasteful in its use of oil and the one which gets the

*The Arctic National Wildlife Refuge in Alaska, an area the Bush administration would like to open to commercial oil exploration to help alleviate the energy crisis.*

fewest miles per gallon from its cars. Japan, for example, uses oil twice as efficiently as does the United States. This nation is also the main contributor to global warming, mostly because of the vast amounts of carbon dioxide spewed into the atmosphere from auto exhausts. Each car in the United States annually emits more than its own weight in carbon dioxide.

The Bush administration has failed so far to provide strong leadership in the fight to reduce environmental damage through greater fuel efficiency. The Department of Energy, which is responsible for the national energy strategy, bowed to White House pressure to protect the auto industry in its December 1990 report on air pollution in the United States and failed to mention higher mileage requirements for cars. White House chief of staff John Sununu repeatedly insisted that conservation concerns must play no role in the nation's energy policy, leading Energy Action, a consumer advocacy group, to lament that George Bush's energy plans "point to a policy that will reward and placate entrenched energy interests."

Despite the influence of such energy interests, there is renewed interest among foreign automakers in fuel conservation and the wise use of nonrenewable resources. High-mileage minicars, such as the Daihatsu Charade, which averages nearly 42 miles per gallon (MPG), are attracting consumer attention. Suzuki Motors reports a sharp increase in sales of its 1991 Suzuki Swift, capable of 48 MPG. Honda Motor Company has a re-designed 1992 Civic Hatchback VX which is able to average 65 MPG on the highway, a 25% increase in gasoline savings from the previous model.

If the current average of 27 MPG for American-made autos was raised to 40 MPG, U.S. oil consumption could be reduced by 2.8 million barrels a day by the year 2005. The automotive technology required to produce this change is already available, although only prototype vehicles are currently being tested. In Germany, the company that produces the Audi is planning a sedan made of aluminum, to reduce the weight (and therefore the gasoline consumption) of the automobile. BMW and Mercedes-Benz, also in Germany, are experimenting with *catalytic converters* that will eliminate 99% of an auto's pollutants. Some of the experimental cars, which could be on sale in Europe and the United States as early as the mid-1990s, are capable of achieving 70 MPG.

## SAVINGS VERSUS SAFETY

A smaller, more fuel-efficient auto may be more dangerous to drive, however, and safety considerations may force other

*The Suzuki Swift, one of the new generation fuel-efficient automobiles. The 1991 Swift averaged 48 miles per gallon.*

means of energy conservation. According to recent reports from the Insurance Institute for Highway Safety, 11 types of General Motors autos, downsized for reasons of fuel economy, had significantly higher death rates than their larger counterparts. Researchers from Harvard University and the Brookings Institution noted similar findings about the safety of small cars, and predicted that fuel-economy rules could be responsible for the deaths of 3,900 Americans in the 1990s.

Other researchers disagree. The U.S. Public Interest Research Group notes that getting more miles per gallon can be accomplished by aerodynamic styling and other improvements rather than by making cars smaller. The Center for Auto Safety, a U.S. consumer group, says that even small cars can be made safe with air bags and other specialized equipment. Public Citizen, which advocates legislation beneficial to U.S. consumers, reports that small cars that can get up to 50 MPG are safe if they are made of high-strength steel filled with foam. Other fuel-efficient design changes that do not affect size are fuel injection systems; a fourth gear on automatic transmissions to reduce engine speed; and electronic ignition systems. It clearly pays an environmental dividend to increase a car's fuel efficiency because, over a 100,000-mile life, a car getting 18 MPG will deposit 58 tons of $CO_2$ into the air, but a car that gets 45 MPG will deposit only 23 tons.

Although federal attempts at fuel conservation in the United States may get bogged down by hesitant administrations and debates over safety, individual states and local governments can—and do—move faster to put fuel-saving measures into action. Vermont recently announced a statewide energy strategy to reduce by one-third the amount of fossil fuel used within its borders. Part of the plan asks motorists to revise auto use enough to reduce toxic emissions by 12%. Businesses in many major U.S. cities, encouraged by local political decisions, sell bus and train tokens at discounts to their employees and urge people to carpool to work. The transit agency in Minneapolis–St. Paul ran ads during the Persian Gulf crisis that featured a photo of Saddam Hussein and a slogan pleading with motorists to "Stop Pumping Him Up" by wasting oil in cars and take trains instead.

In many densely populated European and Asian cities, the bicycle accounts for most of a citizen's daily trips to work, school, shops, or to visit friends. In Beijing, China, for example, 48% of a person's daily trips are made by bike, and there are 250 bicycles to every auto. In Delft, Netherlands, 43% of daily trips are made on a bike even though there are only 2.2 bikes for every auto. By comparison, 8% of daily trips in Manhattan, in the United States, are made by bicycle and there are 0.7 bikes for every automobile.

Clearly, it will take a national policy of fuel conservation to substantially change the driving habits of Americans. Such a policy may be most effective if it provides for increases in the price of fuel and decreases in the cost of subway and bus tokens. Although the competitive market, and not government rules, determines the cost of fuel in the United States, it is possible for the government to provide for higher fuel costs indirectly by the addition of taxes or by requirements for the development of cleaner fuels.

The revisions to the Clean Air Act passed in 1990 show Congress' determination to safeguard the environment against auto emissions. According to the act, by the year 2000 the cities of Baltimore, Chicago, Hartford, Houston, Los Angeles, Milwaukee, New York, Philadelphia, and San Diego must have

*A Kuwaiti oil field burns out of control after the Persian Gulf war of 1991. Political instability in the Middle East is a big factor in rising energy prices.*

only clean-burning gasolines in their cars. These cities have been labeled by the federal government as the nine smoggiest in the United States. The development of clean fuels will cost drivers 6 to 10 cents more per gallon of gasoline. By 2003, as a result of new fuel conservation technology, new cars will cost American motorists about $600 more. In addition, the act specifies that to save fuel, auto manufacturers in Southern California will have to build several thousand test cars that operate on alternative fuels such as electricity, natural gas, or methanol.

Adding several dollars or more to the price of gasoline is seen by many people as the only real way to force fuel conservation. A survey of cities across the nation during the war in the Persian Gulf showed that a small increase in gasoline prices did not encourage most Americans to abandon their cars in favor of mass transit. While soldiers fought on Middle Eastern deserts for control of oil wells, U.S. citizens continued to use fuel freely. Sy Mouler, a spokesman for the San Francisco Bay Area Rapid Transit system, has claimed that, "If gas hits $2.50 or $2.75 a gallon, then we're going to see people leave their cars." According to the American Automobile Association, the average national price per gallon of unleaded regular fuel at a self-service station was $1.37, as of October 1990.

The SUnSUrfer, built by Stanford University students, is an experimental solar car that holds one driver. Photovoltaic cells cover its rear surface.

# A   D I F F E R E N T   T Y P E
# O F   C A R

In an effort to redesign cars so they will be energy-efficient and still affordable, the auto industry, universities, and other private interests are experimenting with electric cars, solar-powered cars, and even hydrogen-powered cars. Most of these cars are too impractical and expensive at present to be ready for sale to consumers. But battery technology and other sciences have made great strides, and manufacturers expect to be producing a different type of automobile by the mid-1990s.

Some of these different types of autos are in very early stages of development. General Motors Corporation has developed what it calls a "hybrid" van, the HX3, that runs on two electric motors with a small gasoline engine for the onboard generation of electric power. But most alternative forms of personal transportation are built around basic, recurring concepts, such as the electric car.

## THE ELECTRIC CAR

The electric car is perhaps closest to becoming a reality because manufacturers already have extensive experience with lead-acid battery technology. Electric cars would have to be built so that they could be plugged into existing sockets in people's garages. Probably, owners would want to recharge their electric cars during the night, when prices for electrical power are lower. Some researchers are also hoping that new designs for hydrogen-oxygen fuel cells, like those used on spacecraft, will replace lead-acid batteries as a source of power. In the past, fuel cells have been too complex and costly to be a real alternative to the gasoline engine, but recent developments in fuel cell technology may overcome these problems. Scientists argue that such fuel cells would cut down greatly on air pollution because they emit only water vapor.

General Motors, Ford, and Chrysler have formed a joint venture, with the federal government funding half the $100 million yearly budget, to develop long-lasting electric car batteries. The city of Osaka, Japan, has teamed up with several companies in that nation to spend $3.3 million on 10 experimental charging stations for electric cars. Fiat, the Italian car manufacturing company, already has an electric car on the market called the Elettra. But it can travel only 45 miles before needing another charge and costs $22,000. There are strong government incentives in Europe for the development of a practical and safe electric car. In December, 1990, the European Commission adopted strict emission standards that may eventually force the auto industry in Europe to abandon gasoline-powered autos. Already, government officials in Switzerland, Germany, and the Netherlands are talking about banning gas autos in city centers.

The most promising electric car so far, however, was developed in the United States and is being publicized by General Motors as ready for the market in the 1990s. It is the Impact, a sleek and silent auto that can zip from 0 to 60 MPH in 8 seconds. The Impact can go 120 miles before needing a re-charge, says GM, and it has a charger that can be plugged into a standard wall outlet. This electric car is made mostly of alumi-num, so it weighs only 2,200 pounds (including 32 lead-acid batteries built into the center tunnel of the chassis). Although GM will not yet reveal the car's projected price, some auto experts worry that it might cost about $20,000. That price would limit its availability for many drivers.

Government studies show that in the United States alone about 95% of all daily trips are well within the range of a small electric car. People apparently use their cars mostly for quick trips

*General Motors's Impact, an electric car that can be recharged by plug-ging it into an ordinary household electrical outlet. GM hopes to have this vehicle ready for the market in the 1990s.*

to work, school, and shopping, or to visit others in the city; such destinations are often just a few miles from home. The car is often parked at this destination for much of the day. An electric auto could be recharged at any destination, or it could run all day and be charged in the family garage at night.

## HYDROGEN-POWERED CARS

Another possibility for a clean car is one powered by hydrogen. Hydrogen is a fuel that can be produced domestically, thus freeing consumers from dependence on foreign oil. Burning it produces just a little water vapor and small amounts of nitrogen oxide.

Hydrogen is one of the most abundant elements on earth, making it an attractive alternative to gasoline, if ways can be found to safely harness its power. It now takes great amounts of energy to process hydrogen for use in cars, and it would require from 65 to 100 pounds of gaseous hydrogen to get a car as far as it would go on a gallon of gasoline. This makes hydrogen too expensive and bulky for practical use.

Still, the lure of an abundant source of power for autos tempts both governments and private firms to experiment with

*The German car manufacturer Mercedes-Benz is experimenting with a vehicle powered by hydrogen gas. The 230 E pictured here has a top speed of 105 miles per hour and a range of about 75 miles in the city.*

hydrogen cars. The U.S. Department of Energy is spending about $3 million per year on hydrogen research. Japan's Mazda Motor Corporation says it will have a commercially viable hydrogen-powered car by the late 1990s. In Europe, Daimler-Benz and BMW have both built hydrogen "research vehicles." BMW's vehicle was a sedan, and Daimler-Benz built a hydrogen station wagon and also intends to build an experimental hydrogen-powered bus. Both companies claim that hydrogen's reputation as a dangerous fuel is exaggerated. Unlike gasoline, hydrogen has no toxic fumes. It is no more explosive than natural gas, and a hydrogen car would be equipped with electronic sensors to detect potential leaks.

The hydrogen car, like some solar-powered cars, is not yet practical because it would be too big, inefficient, and expensive to run. But since refrigerated liquid hydrogen is three times more powerful than gasoline—and a lot cleaner—it remains a hope for the future.

## THE SOLAR CAR

The future may also see an automobile powered directly by the sun. The key factor in producing such a car is to find ways to cheaply convert sunlight into electricity. Some scientists say a combination of hydrogen fuel and *photovoltaic cells* is the best bet. Dr. John Appleby, director of Texas A & M University's Center for Electrochemical Systems and Hydrogen Research, says hydro-solar cars would be three times as efficient as the present internal combustion auto.

Solar cars are a reality now. Honda has a low, sleek solar car called the Dream. Toyota's Ra-Ra is a solar prototype that

*Toyota's futuristic-looking Ra-Ra is powered by solar energy.*

resembles a landlocked motorboat. Some other solar cars being tested have solar-powered ventilators that cool the car while it is parked, thus cutting the amount of energy needed for air-conditioning when the driver returns.

For the most part, however, today's solar cars are experimental vehicles built by universities. To show that solar power is practical, university teams enter these cars in races, such as the 1,900-mile trans-Australian World Solar Challenge. In November 1990, a team of 120 students from the University of Michigan in Ann Arbor placed third in the challenge with their car, the Sunrunner. The students were mostly majors in electrical engineering, aerospace technology, computer science, and mechanical engineering. There were 35 such competitors in the race, hailing from nine countries.

Sunrunner weighs 503 pounds. It features solar arrays on its sides as well as its top to capture diffuse, reflected *solar energy* in cloudy weather. The car's orientation toward the sun, the charge of its battery, and the intensity of the sunlight were constantly monitored during the race. It achieved an average speed of over 32 MPH.

Like most other experimental solar cars, Sunrunner is small and meant for one person. The SUnSUrfer of Stanford University (which finished seventh in GM's Sun Rayce USA from Orlando, Florida to Detroit, Michigan in 1991) weighs about 600 pounds. Like Sunrunner, it is a long, low, and very sleek futuristic vehicle. Solar cells are placed in a semicylindrical array over the bulk of the car, and its frame is built of fiberglass. The motor weighs 13 pounds.

Solar cars work on energy provided by sunlight. When particles of light hit the materials in solar cells, electrons are released and current begins to flow. The current is channeled to the motor as power or to the storage batteries, which provide power when no sunlight is available.

Standard solar cells are only about 12% efficient. Cells that are about 20% efficient are available, but they are too expensive to be practical. Solar batteries are also heavy, weighing between 50 to 70 pounds, and they are about 20 times as expensive as conventional lead-acid batteries (though they have about 4 times the storage capacity). With these solar batteries, SUnSUrfer is able to cover 200 miles at 30 MPH on a single charge. When the sun is shining brightly, a solar battery generates enough electricity to run indefinitely.

GETTING MORE MILEAGE

Another way of reducing pollution is to build autos that use a lot less gasoline. High-mileage minicars are attracting interest as possible ways to cut down on oil dependence and reduce pollutants. Cars like the Daihatsu Charade and the Suzuki Swift already get 42 to 48 miles to a gallon of gas and have been

*Honda's Dream, a sleek experimental solar vehicle.*

selling well, despite studies by the Insurance Institute for Highway Safety that warn of higher death rates for drivers of smaller cars. There already is legislation in America that says carmakers have to come up with cars that deliver at least 27.5 miles per gallon; some researchers say this can be done with cars that are big enough to be safe if less emphasis is put on power and speed.

Although federal regulations call upon auto manufacturers to supply the public with gas-conserving automobiles, manufacturers have been aided by the administrations of presidents Ronald Reagan and George Bush in delaying and in some cases avoiding the regulations. Recent administrations have believed pushing up the number of miles per gallon a car can achieve is too difficult and expensive, and detrimental to the competitiveness of the U.S. automobile industry, in spite of all the evidence that foreign automakers may soon be putting even more fuel-efficient cars into the American market.

Techniques for increasing fuel efficiency include limiting top speeds, using front-wheel drive, having extra intake and exhaust valves, and improving aerodynamic styling. Individuals can often get better fuel efficiency in the cars they now own simply by balancing their tires to decrease road friction and by cutting down on the use of auto air conditioners.

Because of recent changes in the Clean Air Act, the price of most new automobiles will probably rise at least $600 by the year 2003. By that year, according to the act, cars will have to emit 60% less nitrogen oxide and 40% less unburned hydro- carbons than is currently allowable. In cities such as Baltimore, Chicago, Houston, Los Angeles, and New York, which are among the smoggiest in the United States, auto drivers may also have to pay more for cleaner-burning gasolines. Patterns of auto use may also have to change. In Southern California, for example, businesses which employ more than 100 people must submit plans to the government detailing ways they will help their employees reduce one car–one person commuting. Under this legislation, known as the South Coast Air Quality Management Plan, employers who continue to allow environmentally damag- ing automobile use for business travel will face stiff fines.

*Pedaling down Fifth Avenue in New York City on Earth Day, commuters prove that the bicycle is a viable alternative to the automobile.*

chapter   6


# A L T E R N A T I V E S   T O
# T H E   A U T O M O B I L E


Finding alternatives to the auto may be one of the most crucial environment-saving tasks of the 1990s. This does not mean that automobiles as a form of transportation must be abandoned completely. The problem is not that people use cars, but that they *overuse* them. A lot of the environmental damage caused by the automobile would be eased if people limited the use of cars to special situations, to rural travel, and to transport passengers, such as disabled persons, who cannot conveniently use public transportation. For everyday travel, such as commuting to work, it would be best for the environment if people selected other methods of getting around.


## W A L K I N G

The most obvious—and most avoided—method of getting around is walking. Because overuse of the automobile quickly degrades the quality of life in cities, and because it is easiest to walk in a city (if proper sidewalks, lighting, and security are provided) many urban planners are calling for renewed efforts to make city streets more "pedestrian-friendly." It is essential to regulate and limit auto use along routes where people wish to walk, because with their mass and speed cars will automatically dominate the space and make foot travel unpleasant and unsafe.

Such regulation is common in Europe, where planners routinely provide for pedestrian use of urban space. Car barriers are placed along routes reserved for walkers, particularly in residential neighborhoods. This is known as "traffic calming." The Dutch, for example, have used traffic calming for 20 years as a way of reclaiming city streets for pedestrians and bicyclists; such streets are known as *woonerf*, or "living yards." Cars are not necessarily banned in the woonerf (although in some cases they are), but they are forced to move slowly around trees, land-scaping, and other carefully placed barriers. The cars are also restricted to narrow lanes, leaving most of the woonerf free for walking, cycling, chatting with neighbors, and children's play. Traffic calming was started in the 1970s in West Germany and has spread rapidly because it makes neighborhoods and small business districts so much more pleasant than car-dominated areas. Sweden, Italy, Switzerland, and Japan are all in the process of adopting the woonerf idea.

Pedestrian traffic is beneficial not only to neighborhoods but to commercial districts as well. Every major European city which has devoted at least part of its core area to pedestrians reports increased sales in shops located in those areas. After pedestrian zones were created recently in the United Kingdom, business in those zones increased 25%. In Lima, Peru, the establishment of pedestrian streets attracted businesses, which in turn attracted more people on foot. After restrictions on autos in

Paris for the 1989 bicentennial of the French Revolution drew many pedestrians and increased business dramatically, Mayor Jacques Chirac ordered the permanent removal of 100,000 parking spaces in the city. He announced that the space would be devoted to people on foot, partly because that was so much better for business.

Travel on foot is essential for many people in non-industrialized parts of the world because so few of them own automobiles, or even bicycles, and they cannot afford public transit. In Third World nations, it has been estimated that one-fourth of the people walk because public transit is too expensive for them. In China, some local governments pay commuters to walk or bicycle to work to relieve overcrowding on buses, and in India and Ghana walking to work is applauded as healthy and even patriotic because it helps cut down on pollution.

Some U.S. cities are experimenting with "walkers only" rules for the city center on holidays and weekends. Atlanta, Georgia, has closed its huge Piedmont Park to all auto traffic on weekends to allow greater freedom, safety, and cleaner air for joggers and picnickers. New York City prohibits autos in Central Park and Prospect Park on Saturdays and Sundays. In Boston, large tracts of city land are permanently devoted to walkways and pedestrian malls near amphitheaters, museums, entertainment areas, and shopping centers where auto traffic is impossible and walking is the only available transportation. Other areas in Boston are closed to auto traffic on weekends to give downtown shoppers more room to roam safely from store to store.

Most modern U.S. city planners realize the value of encouraging people to walk. But because this country has evolved as an auto-dependent nation, many of its cities bow to the demands of drivers and fail to encourage pedestrian use of urban space until overcrowding, decay, and pollution become intense. In some cities, such as Dallas and Phoenix, street configurations are often geared for cars instead of people, so it takes a great deal of restructuring, and a lot of city money, to lure walkers back into the streets.

### BICYCLE RIDING

When walking is not possible, the next best alternative to auto travel is bicycle commuting. Like the auto, bikes provide virtually door-to-door convenience, but unlike the automobile they are nonpolluting.

There are 800 million bicycles in the world, and each year 100 million more of them are made. That is about three times the number of autos manufactured each year. Most of the world's bicycles are in Asia, with China alone claiming about 300 million of them, 1 for every 4 people. Bikes in Asia transport more people than all of the world's autos combined, and in many developing nations bicycles are used to carry produce and other goods to and from the marketplace; thus bikes are important to those nation's economies. In China and Japan, cycling to work is encouraged as a matter of public policy as a way to reduce pollution and overcrowding on public transit. The government of the former Soviet Union encouraged bicycle riding as a way to fight air pollution and sponsored extensive bicycle paths in many of its member states, a practice that will hopefully continue in the sovereign republics. The Netherlands, regarded as the most "bike-friendly" industrialized nation, gives broad support to people who choose to cycle in and around its cities. In parts of

Australia the mail is delivered by bicycle, and Kenyan dairy farmers bring milk to customer's doorsteps on bicycles.

Although people in highly industrialized nations own many bicycles, few use them on a regular basis for anything but recreation. In Great Britain, for example, 1 in 4 people owns a bicycle but only about 1 trip out of 33 is made by bicycle. This is in spite of the fact that the glut of cars in Britain's large cities often brings life there to a standstill. In 1989, London set the world record for traffic jams when it had cars backed up from the city center on its highways for 33 miles.

There are also a lot of bikes in the United States—virtually everyone in the nation owns a bicycle at one time or another—but only 1 out of 40 bikes in the United States are used to commute to work. Part of the reason is that while Asian and European nations plan for bicycles with special pathways and bicycle parking areas, American transit planners are generally accustomed to thinking in terms of auto travel only. Also, one out of every two Americans owns a car, so bicycle travel is rarely a necessity. U.S. residents are therefore accustomed to thinking of the bicycle as a vehicle only for children or for adult recreational use.

Gradually, however, bicycle riding as a way to get to work and to shopping is taking hold. In resort areas such as Cape Cod in Massachusetts and Hilton Head in South Carolina, bicycle transportation was originally planned mainly as recreation for tourists but became woven into the fabric of the community as residents recognized the pleasant quality of life that bike transportation makes possible. In 1980, the city of Chicago did a transportation analysis and announced that the most cost-effective way of reducing its urban pollution was to get people to mass-transit stations by bicycle. When the Clean Air Act was revised in

1989, over 40 U.S. cities included bike promotion measures as a way to reduce air pollution.

A recent study has shown that for every commuter in the United States who gets to public transit by bike instead of car, about 150 gallons of gas are saved per year. If only 10% of all Americans who now commute by car changed instead to riding a bike to public transit, the U.S. oil import bill would drop by $1 billion annually.

## PUBLIC BUSES

Unlike trains, buses as a form of public transport require no special street configurations or modifications. This makes bus transportation an easily implemented alternative to the auto-

*This modern electric street car in Buffalo, New York, is one of a number of vehicles designed to ease inner-city transportation problems.*

mobile; it may take years to build a subway or monorail, but city officials can set up new bus routes in days.

Buses are also a safe alternative to the car. A rider has 97 times the chance of being killed in an auto as he has riding in a bus. Buses are also much cheaper than cars. Counting gas, maintenance, insurance, depreciation, and other hidden costs of auto ownership, it costs at least $34 to go 100 miles in a car compared to about $14 to go 100 miles in a bus. Auto travelers must also bear the cost and frustration of having to find a parking spot for the car at the end of a trip.

Most Americans are familiar with the conventional city bus. But these public vehicles come in many forms: minibus, double-decker, trolley bus, and even the "bending bus," which is twice as long as a conventional bus and has a pivoting center to help it bend around curves in the street. People enjoy bus travel for its convenience and low cost, as well for as the ability to see where they are going, in contrast to the monotonous view of an underground rail corridor. In many parts of the world where government-sponsored bus systems cannot meet the demand for public transit, privately run minivans, minibuses, and medium-sized buses make money by filling the gap. In the United States, private bus systems such as Greyhound have long provided swift and affordable travel between cities and within sprawling suburban areas.

A bus emits 189 grams of carbon monoxide per passenger-kilometer, compared to 934 grams of carbon monoxide emitted by an automobile to carry 1 person the same distance. In addition, buses can carry over 30,000 people in 1 lane per hour while cars move only 8,000 people in the same space in 1 hour.

Buses account for 20% to 30% of all city travel in a typical European city and up to 80% of all motorized trips in Asia, Latin America, and Africa. This contrasts with a bus ridership of only about 5% for commuters in U.S. cities, again primarily because of a mindset geared toward automobile use. It is not uncommon for buses in many other parts of the world to be crowded and uncomfortable. In Indonesia, for example, and many other nations, it is common to see people clinging to the sides of packed buses. Yet citizens use them because they either do not own automobiles or because they have been socially conditioned to think in terms of mass transit.

Bus use in the United States is slowly gaining favor, however, as city officials search for ways to relieve congestion and comply with clean-air standards. New York City leads the way for bus use in the United States; nearly one-quarter of the nation's bus trips are logged there. Other cities, seeking to implement safe, convenient, affordable public transit quickly, could emulate that city's excellent bus service.

## TAKING THE TRAIN

Trains come in many forms. They go underground through tunnels or overhead on elevated tracks. Streetcars on rails are called trams, and some cities still use the electric trolley, which looks like a quaint bus hooked to a system of wires that criss-cross the streets to provide power. There are also city-to-city or regional trains.

When it comes to saving the environment, trains come out far ahead of autos and even buses. They don't spew out carbon monoxide or gulp gas, and a vehicle on a rapid rail system

Japan's Shinkansen, *or "bullet trains," are the fastest in the world, with speeds of more than 125 miles per hour. They are a highly efficient alternative to the automobile.*

can move 60 people using six times less energy than it takes for an auto to move 1 person. A train corridor also takes up much less space than does a road, which means there is less concrete and asphalt to deface the cities. Trains can carry about 70,000 people on a single track in one hour, but it takes about nine lanes to carry that many people by auto in the same amount of time, even if every auto has four people in it.

The ideal method of commuting in big cities is riding a bike to the train station, taking the bike on the train, then biking again to the office door. Recognizing this, bike-riding groups in

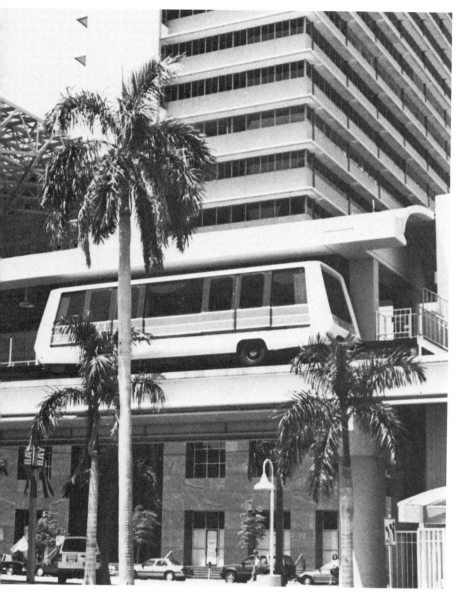

In Miami, Florida, a new system of wheeled buses roll along on elevated tracks.

the United States are pressuring cities with rapid rail lines to allow people to wheel their bikes into designated sections of the train. It is not unusual to see bike riders in Europe shouldering their bicycles to get through rush hour on the subway or metro system. Japan has pioneered fast, efficient train travel with its bullet trains, or *Shinkansen*, which zoom through cities at 200 miles per hour.

Trains are so easy to ride and so much better for the environment than auto transit that many American cities are expanding their rail systems now to prepare for future needs. In Miami, Florida, a new monorail goes to the airport from various business centers. San Diego, California, is expanding its trolley system. Even in Los Angeles, a city known for its reckless love affair with the auto, and which has two-thirds of its urban space paved over for parking lots, a new, 150-mile rapid rail system is being built.

City planners now realize that time is running out for finding nonpolluting alternatives to the automobile. Trains seem to offer the best hope for city transportation that is also compatible with the environment.

*Heavy traffic on Interstate 270 in Maryland. In many areas of the country, highways no longer serve their intended function of moving vehicles rapidly from one point to another.*

chapter 7

# THE BIG ROADS

Where there are cars, there must be roads upon which they can travel. The big roads, constructed with massive funding from federal and state sources, are known as highways, expressways, or interstates. They all have the same purpose: to move autos swiftly from point to point, in as straight a path as possible. And they all tend to cause great environmental disruption.

Thirty-five years ago, when President Dwight Eisenhower announced a plan to develop an interlocking highway system for interstate travel, protection of the natural environment was a minor concern. People were far more interested in the rewards of highways—speed, access, ease of travel, and commercial development—than they were in air, water, noise, and visual pollution. Now, however, environmental degradation has been added to a long list of other highway woes, including the fact that in many cases they no longer work. Almost as soon as it is built, a highway becomes congested, because creating roads also lures more cars. Thus, building a highway almost ensures traffic jams, because the highway encourages overuse of the automobile. Very soon there is pressure from roadbuilders and frustrated drivers to build again and to repeat the cycle.

The U.S. General Accounting Office says that Americans spend 2 billion hours a year stalled in highway traffic, and if auto use continues unabated, traffic congestion on the nation's big roads will triple in 15 years. In 1 year, American drivers waste 3 billion gallons of oil in highway traffic congestion, 4% of the nation's annual gas consumption. The average speed on a U.S. interstate is a crawl of less than 35 MPH, but that's far better than in Rome, where a car can usually go no faster than 6 MPH during rush hour. In Bangkok, the rush hour pace is about 3 MPH on their best highways, and in Tokyo it is not unusual to be stuck without moving on the highway for 8 to 10 hours. The big roads, which were supposed to be the auto owner's ticket to freedom, have instead become a prison.

## "SMART" HIGHWAYS

Because building more roads is so destructive, and because the United States has already completed its interstate system of 42,797 miles for a cost of over $122 billion, traffic experts are looking for ways to make existing highways work better. One way to do this is by computerizing major traffic arteries with communications networks that will show drivers the best route to travel with a video map on the car's dashboard. In some cases a computer-generated voice would warn the driver of an accident up ahead and recommend another route. Sensors along such a "smart" highway would keep cars at a safe distance from one another, and individualized identification codes in each auto could be recorded at toll stations so drivers could zip through and be billed at the end of the month.

A modified version of this system, called Guidestar, is being planned for 300 miles of highway in Minnesota and could be in place by 1995. Pathfinder, in Santa Monica, California, is a $2.5 million experimental project along 14 miles of the Santa Monica Freeway that uses closed-circuit television to advise motorists of the safest and quickest routes to their destination. New York and New Jersey are starting research on developing smart highways in their areas, and the city of Orlando, Florida, recently signed an agreement with General Motors and the American Automobile Association to build a smart highway for Orlando. The system, called TravTek (for Travel Technology), will provide drivers with traffic information and route selection.

Smart highways are close to reality in Tokyo, where a project sponsored by the Japanese government and 50 automotive and electronics companies is producing a "moving map" for every driver. A color map of Tokyo is displayed on a computer screen near the driver's seat, and a touch of the button causes a yellow arrow to trace the best route over the map. Cities in France, Germany, and Italy will have smart highways by 1992, owing to a billion-dollar investment by 5 governments, 14 automotive companies, and 70 electronics firms.

Even with smart highway technology, experts on the environment warn that congestion and pollution will worsen all over the world in coming years. Michael Renner, a senior researcher at the Worldwatch Institute, says that smart highways cannot solve the problem of "too many cars for roads that can't be built fast enough." He and others concerned with the environment suggest that along with smart highways, planners develop programs for carpooling, mass-transit systems, flexible work hours to stagger the times commuters will have to travel, and "road pricing," or making motorists pay for the time they spend driving on a highway.

### HIGHWAY POLLUTION

"Smart" or otherwise, highways disturb the environment. During construction, great mounds of earth are moved, and native vegetation is stripped and replaced with concrete. Streams are rerouted or covered over, and water is polluted with construction materials. Worn tires, shreds of rubber, lost hubcaps, junked autos, soft-drink cans, and the remnants of carry-out snacks are just some of the objects that create litter along the route of a highway.

Another very apparent effect of highway building is the destruction of trees. By mowing down and burning trees, highway builders not only release waste materials into the air during the construction process, but they also remove one of earth's great natural air-purifying systems. Trees cleanse carbon dioxide from the air, and their loss to highway construction, along with the concentration of autos along the highway corridor, worsens the air for miles in every direction. The huge trucks that rumble along highways spew out a deadly concentration of diesel exhaust. Scientists at the Baylor College of Medicine in Houston, Texas, think that diesel exhaust contains chemicals that can alter the body's DNA, changing the way cells behave and possibly leading to the growth of cancerous tumors. Dr. Kurt Randerath, Baylor's chief of toxicology, says that the relationship between diesel exhaust and cancer is the same that scientists saw when they first studied links between cigarettes and cancer in the 1960s.

Landscaping along highways is one way to offset the air pollution brought on by these massive projects. Although the replanting of trees along highway corridors is usually left to the goodwill and the budget of state and local transportation departments, private industries are now beginning to realize that tree planting is a good way to mitigate some of the destructive effects of a highway and earn the praises of the public at the same time. In some states, both large and small companies can "adopt" stretches of highway, which they promise to plant with trees and maintain.

## UNWANTED LIGHT AND NOISE

Light pollution, or the presence of unwanted or overly bright lights in an area where they do not belong, often affects

*Visual pollution along a surburban road. Much of American culture and commerce is now designed to attract the automobile driver.*

people who live as many as three or four city blocks from a highway. The constant stream of headlights, plus the intrusive glare from overhead safety lamps, impinges upon the peace and privacy of residents. Highway lights are also a major factor in the death of wildlife along these corridors; animals are blinded by the glare of oncoming headlights, freeze in panic, and are run over by cars. Every traveler along a highway is familiar with the grim sight of the crushed bodies of rabbits, raccoons, turtles, birds, snakes, and even deer that try to cross a highway and cannot escape the confusion of headlights. Along some beaches in Georgia, hundreds of endangered baby loggerhead turtles confuse the lights from highways with the soft reflection of the moon on the water. Instead of emerging from the sand at night and crawling into the sea—as they have been programmed by nature to do—the newly hatched turtles crawl toward the highway and are crushed by traffic.

Noise pollution is another serious environmental problem near highways. Steady traffic produces a deep, droning hum that makes normal conversation difficult and makes it hard to concentrate. Stop-and-go traffic may be even worse. Noise pollution is one problem that must be considered by transportation planners before a highway is built. To comply with the National Environmental Policy Act and other federal and state regulations, traffic noise analyses are required. To find out what the "worst hour" traffic noise would be like, computers are used to predict highway sounds based on vehicles traveling at constant speeds. Specialized computer programs can also tell planners what the noise level will be like when cars and trucks accelerate and decelerate.

Research on highway traffic noise levels is carried out by the Transportation Research Board, the American Association of

State Highway and Transportation Officials, and the Federal Highway Administration. They use their findings to help determine the design of a particular highway or to figure out where to place noise-retaining "berms," or walls. Critics of these groups (who are usually environmentalists opposed to highway building) say that road construction should be stopped if projected noise levels would be incompatible with the peaceful everyday pursuits of nearby residents, such as reading or playing the piano.

HIGHWAY HISTORY

Since the beginning of the big road concept, there have been people who opposed rampant highway building, especially in urban areas. However, the history of highways shows a federal mind-set in favor of auto transit, particularly when it comes to spending vast sums of the taxpayers' money.

The first federal aid for highways, the Federal Aid Road Act of 1916, was a program to build rural roads. It was administered through the Department of Agriculture and was seen as one way to help farmers transport their goods to market by trucks. In 1941 a presidential committee recommended a system of national highways to improve state-to-state transportation and to meet civil defense needs in case U.S. soldiers had to be quickly transported from one area to the next.

The answer was the Federal Aid Highway Act of 1944. Engineers were no longer content to build narrow strips of concrete in small towns and farming centers; now they envisioned highways that would link together huge urban areas via the automobile. The act of 1944 would create a national system of interstate highways, setting aside $125 million per year for big

*Building ever more highways is not proving to be the answer to traffic congestion, but it does consume land that might be used for agriculture or housing.*

roads. By 1947, 37,700 miles of this system had been designated, and there were 41,000 miles of it by 1964.

By 1956, when another Federal Aid Highway Act went into effect, the amount of money being spent on U.S. highways was $1 billion per year. The new act specified that money for such projects should come mainly from gasoline taxes. This system now costs over $50 billion per year, with the federal government paying 90% of the cost of an interstate highway system and 10% paid by the states. An interstate can cost from $10 million to $30 million per mile, depending on the cost of acquiring and clearing the right-of-way, demolishing buildings, relocating public utilities, blasting for tunnels, and building overpasses and bridges.

Since the early 1930s, when auto ownership began to boom, both state and federal governments solved traffic problems by building more roads. Most citizens were grateful for the roads, which were seen as golden avenues to development in rural areas and as pathways to the peaceful countryside by people stuck in the city.

However, the 1930s also spawned regional planners such as Benton MacKaye, the man who dreamed up the idea of the Appalachian Trail. He worried that highways could weaken human values because they destroyed the natural environment and encouraged people to move farther and farther away from the city center and its culture. MacKaye warned that highways would bring a future of single-family homes on cheap land in the suburbs, where people would flee in the evening to "escape" the city. The result, he knew, would be an almost slavish dependence on the automobile.

MacKaye proposed, instead, using highways as funnels for autos to a landscaped parking lot, where they could leave the car and continue their journey to town on trains and buses. He also pushed the idea of bike trails to mass-transit stations, so workers and schoolchildren could commute by bike. His ideas, generally disregarded in those early days of auto travel, are being revived now.

In the 1950s and 1960s, transportation expert and city planner Wilfred Owen pointed out that highways "pollute" neighborhoods through which they run and contribute to urban decay. Because highways spur what is known as *ribbon development,* they encourage townships built along their route to be strung-out and formless, with no city center or sense of community. Commercial development near highways tends to be auto-dependent, producing fast-food shops and gasoline stations. This unsightly development, said Owen, erodes the value of nearby residential properties, and the "ribbon" turns into blight.

Another important critic of highways was Lewis Mumford, a world-renowned planner and architect who denounced the United States' dependence on the automobile as a main reason why many U.S. cities are congested and ugly. In their zeal to lay out a concrete path for automobiles, said Mumford, highway engineers forgot about nature's beauty and the frailty of the environment. In his book *The Highway and the City*, Mumford wrote, "In many parts of the country the building of a highway has about the same result upon vegetation and human structures as the passage of a tornado or the blast of an atom bomb....Since the engineer regards his own work as more important than the other human functions it serves, he does not hesitate to lay waste to woods, streams, parks, and human neighborhoods in order to carry his roads straight to their supposed destination."

## THE STORY OF GEORGIA 400

One example of Mumford's worst fears is Georgia 400, a six-lane, six-and-one-quarter-mile tollway that cuts through the heart of urban Atlanta. The road had been on the drawing board since the late 1960s, but the objections of civic and conservation groups, plus heavy neighborhood opposition, blocked its construction. As the city grew and residents questioned the wisdom of building a highway to jam more autos into an already over-crowded downtown, Georgia 400 became synonymous with environmental destruction.

The story of this road shows that the threat of such destruction, however, is often overshadowed by politics and greed. Building Georgia 400 would result in cutting a 95-foot swath through an established single-family neighborhood, destroying at least 145 homes and businesses and bulldozing 290 acres of old-growth forests with a loss of 42,000 trees. These were facts that nobody denied but that many chose to ignore. Pressure for building the road came from a variety of business owners who saw profits in road-building projects and from politicians who felt too insecure to oppose these powerful interests. Although many local leaders sided with neighborhood activists in opposing the road at first, one by one the politicians caved in and switched sides. After nearly 20 years of wrangling between those who were eager to build the road and those who understood its potential for environmental destruction, Georgia 400 was built. The projected savings in time from home to office for auto commuters is five minutes.

The sad lesson of Georgia 400 is that highways have such enormous impact on the politics and economics of a region that common sense and factual information are often not enough to coax officials away from overdependence on auto transport and big roads. The citizens who opposed Georgia 400 mounted a concerted, sustained effort to switch Atlanta from an auto city to a pedestrian and mass-transit city. They failed largely because developers and road builders had more money and more political clout. Although Georgia 400 was built, conservation-minded citizens came very close to achieving their goal. Perhaps they set the stage for greater environmental awareness in Atlanta, and in other major U.S. cities, in the future.

*New traffic regulations will compel drivers to use their cars more efficiently. On this road, people are required to carpool.*

chapter 8

# BECOMING A BETTER DRIVER

All cars pollute the environment, but many people
cannot, or will not, abandon the automobile. It is possible,
however, to be a more environmentally aware driver, and thus
help to substantially reduce the pollution now caused by cars.
The way a car is driven affects the number of miles that can be
squeezed from a gallon of gas. Since fuel use is highly polluting,
each gallon saved helps curb environmental damage. Thus
driving habits play a substantial role in regulating pollution
caused by each individual automobile.

Smooth driving means more miles per gallon. Quick starts
and racing from stop light to stop light guarantee low gas mileage.
Gradual acceleration and deceleration save gas, and so does
using cruise control only on long trips where the car is traveling
on flat, open roads. This is because the constant engaging and
disengaging of the cruise control mechanism uses up gasoline.
Revving the car engine just before shutting it off is also wasteful
of gas, and it is totally unnecessary—so is idling the engine. A car
will warm up after about five minutes of driving, even on the
coldest days.

Another big gas user is an auto's air-conditioning unit. Some people try to save gas by turning the air conditioner off and opening windows. This well-meaning gesture may, however, increase the car's "drag factor" and use more gas. Since most air-conditioning units in modern automobiles have a variety of settings, experts recommend setting the unit on "normal" or "low" and opening the windows slightly. This will keep the auto's interior cool without increasing wind resistance.

It is important when planning auto trips to combine many errands in one outing, rather than using a car several different times. If possible, avoid car trips in the city by walking, bicycle riding, or taking mass transit instead. Carpooling is also an enormous help to the environment; obviously, the fewer cars on the road, the less pollution.

The weight of a car is another factor in how much gas it uses. Every 100 pounds removed from an automobile increases that car's efficiency by slightly over 1%. It is therefore less polluting if non-essential items are removed from the auto. The only important items that should be in a car trunk are a spare tire, a jack, an emergency light, and repair tools.

PROPER MAINTENANCE

The EPA, recognizing that a poorly tuned car uses about 10% more gasoline than one that is well maintained, recommends annual tune-ups for any auto built before 1981. Models made after 1981 need annual inspections but may not require a tune-up every year.

On fuel-injected engines, it is important that the air filter be clean because fuel and air are mixed very precisely and the flow of air determines how much gasoline is used. The use of high-octane gasoline with detergent additives helps keep fuel injectors clean, and less gas is used.

Dragging brakes can substantially reduce fuel efficiency, so keeping a car's brakes adjusted will help the environment. Oil should be changed regularly because clean engine oil ensures maximum efficiency and gas savings, and so does the use of a high-quality multigrade oil. If an auto's wheels are out of alignment fuel is wasted, so wheel alignment should be checked regularly.

Under-inflated tires decrease gas mileage by at least 5%. The EPA estimates that 65 million cars on American roads have tires which are not properly inflated, and the sheer numbers involved make a significant contribution to global warming. The EPA says that up to 17 million tons of carbon dioxide are dumped into the atmosphere each year because of under-inflated tires.

*Minivans like this one in New York City carry a lot of commuters for the gasoline they consume and are efficient people-movers.*

The correct pressure for any automobile tire is determined by the manufacturer and included in the car owner's manual. Tires should also be balanced for maximum mileage. Some auto experts say that radial tires not only last longer but can improve gas mileage by 5% in the city and by 7% on the highway. Radials should not be matched with conventional tires unless the owner's manual specifies that this is appropriate.

When tires are worn out, it is more beneficial to the environment to recycle them as playground gear or garden borders than to toss them in a dump. Environmental engineers are also conducting experiments with discarded tires to see if they can be used in systems to clean up wastewater from food processing plants. The old tires, which would be rescued from dumpsters, highways, and individual owners, could be shredded and installed as microbe catchers in anaerobic wastewater systems. These systems clean water by degrading wastes into combustible gases. Plastic is now used as the microbe catcher in such systems, but if the plastic could be replaced by rubber tires the process would be cheaper and would provide a way to recycle the tires on a larger scale.

## AUTOMOTIVE WASTE DISPOSAL

The average automobile contains many hazardous materials. When it's time to dispose of them, those materials can quickly turn into toxins that poison the earth, the air, and contaminate water supplies. Disposing of these materials properly takes planning, patience, and extra work.

The most damaging fluids in a car are antifreeze, battery acid, transmission fluid, used oil, and brake fluid. Brake fluid, transmission fluid, and used oil are all toxic and flammable. Antifreeze is toxic. The lead and sulfuric acid from auto batteries is both toxic and corrosive.

None of these fluids should be poured down a drain or into sewers. If used oil is kept clean, it will probably be accepted by a neighborhood garage for recycling. If the garage cannot recycle the fluids, it may have special, environmentally safe containers in which to dispose of the materials. Be sure to take the materials to the garage in heavy containers which have well-fitted lids.

Used antifreeze can also be poured into a sturdy container with a tight lid and taken to local service stations for disposal. Some stations will put the antifreeze into storage drums. If this cannot be done, antifreeze can be diluted with generous amounts of water, then poured into a gravel pit or a similar area with good drainage. The toxic ingredient in antifreeze is glycol, which is poisonous to fish and wildlife. It will also kill family pets and youngsters who may be tempted into sampling the sweet-tasting fluid. Keep animals away from antifreeze and make sure it is far from the reach of curious children.

Two other dangerous materials are lead and sulfuric acid, both of which are found in car batteries. When burned, the lead in the batteries pollutes the air. If buried in landfills, car batteries leak lead that fouls the soil and seeps into groundwater supplies. Batteries can be recycled, however. This is routine in Europe and Japan but is still a new concept in the United States. Eighty million car batteries are discarded each year in the United States. Auto batteries can be recycled if brought to service stations that know how to do this; at the very least, the station should be able to offer safe disposal. Some local governments are now beginning

*The Honda CRX HF is the highest-mileage four cylinder car available on the American market, getting about 50 miles per gallon. Newer Hondas are rumored to get 100 miles per gallon of gasoline.*

to require deposits on car batteries so drivers will not throw them away. In Suffolk County, New York, there is a $5 refund on auto batteries, which has been effective in keeping the toxic materials from such batteries out of the local water and soil.

### SMART AUTO SHOPPING

Buying a car that delivers good gas mileage is easy on the environment and the pocketbook. Cars that deliver superior mileage include the Geo Metro XFI (55 MPG); the Honda Civic CRX HF (50 MPG); the Suzuki Swift (48 MPG); and the Daihatsu Charade (39 MPG). These numbers are for basic autos without automatic transmission or air-conditioning.

Cars with air-conditioning release CFCs, or chlorofluorocarbons, into the atmosphere. According to the EPA, the CFCs in American cars account for about 20% of the damage to the ozone layer. The best remedy is to do without air-conditioning if possible. In hot climates where driving without air-conditioning is just too uncomfortable, it is best for auto owners to have their air-conditioning units kept in top shape so CFCs leak as little as possible.

Recharging a car's coolant is of no use. If the system needs to be recharged, it indicates a leak of CFCs; recharging does not repair the leak. Responsible service stations will not recharge a leaking air-conditioning system without repairing it. Many auto owners submit to annual recharging without realizing that this is a sham and of no use to either the car owner or the environment. The appropriate method of servicing an auto air-conditioning unit is to capture and recycle CFCs without leaking them into the air.

If a car has automatic transmission, it should also have a fourth gear to reduce engine speeds and increase fuel economy. Since wind resistance uses fuel, the shape of a car can affect its mileage. The less wind resistance offered by the car's shape, the better it will be for the environment. Pointed, low, and sleek shapes allow cars to slice through the air more efficiently, with less resistance than big, boxy designs. One of the advantages of the GM Impact, an experimental electric car, is its teardrop shape and low, sleek lines. It has a sloped front end and "skirts" that cover about half of the rear wheels. This gives the Impact a drag coefficient of 0.19, which is 34% better than any conventional car on the market today. Cars with darkened or tinted windows are also preferable, because the darker interior stays cooler and thus requires less air-conditioning.

# APPENDIX: FOR MORE INFORMATION

## Environmental Organizations

Air Pollution Control Association
P.O. Box 2861
Pittsburgh, PA 15230
(412) 578-8111

Alternative Sources of Energy,
   Inc.
107 South Central Avenue
Milaca, MN 56353

American Automobile
   Association (AAA)
8111 Gatehouse Road
Falls Church, VA 22047
(703) 222-6000

American Council for an Energy
   Efficient Economy
1001 Connecticut Avenue NW,
   Suite 535
Washington, DC 20013
(202) 429-8873

American Lung Association
1740 Broadway
New York, NY 10019
(212) 315-8700

Center for Clean Air Policy
444 North Capitol Street
Washington, DC 20001
(202) 624-7709

Environmental Defense Fund
257 Park Avenue South
New York, NY 10010
(212) 505-2100

Global Tomorrow Coalition
1325 G Street NW
Washington, DC 20005-3014
(202) 628-4016

National Clean Air Coalition
530 Seventh Street SE
Washington, DC 20003
(202) 543-8200

Natural Resources Defense
   Council
40 West 20th Street
New York, NY 10011
(212) 727-2700

Pollution Probe Foundation
12 Madison Avenue
Toronto, Ontario M5R 2S1
Canada
(416) 926-1907

Renewable Fuels Association
201 Massachusetts Avenue NW
Washington, DC 20002
(202) 543-3802

World Resources Institute
1735 New York Avenue NW
Washington, DC 20006
(202) 638-6300

Worldwatch Institute
1776 Massachusetts Avenue NW
Washington, DC 20036
(202) 452-1999

## Government Organizations

Council on Environmental
  Quality
722 Jackson Place NW
Washington, DC 20006
(202) 395-5750

Department of Energy
Forrestal Building
1000 Independence Avenue SW
Washington, DC 20585
(202) 586-5000

Department of Transportation
400 Seventh Street SW
Washington, DC 20590
(202) 366-4000

Environmental Protection Agency
401 M Street SW
Washington, DC 20460
(202) 382-2080

United Nations Environment
  Program
North American Liaison Office
Room DC 2-0803
United Nations, NY 10017
(212) 963-8093

# FURTHER READING

Appleyard, Donald. *Livable Streets.* Berkeley: University of California Press, 1981.

Brown, Lester R. *State of the World.* New York: Norton, 1991.

Creighton, Roger L. *Urban Transportation Planning.* Champaign: University of Illinois Press, 1970.

Elkington, John, et al. *The Green Consumer.* New York: Penguin Books, 1991.

Grad, Frank P., et al. *The Automobile and the Regulation of its Impact on the Environment.* Norman: University of Oklahoma Press, 1974.

Kovarik, Bill. *Fuel Alcohol: Energy and Environment in a Hungry World.* Washington, DC: Earthscan, 1982.

Lewis, David L., and Laurence Goldstein. *The Automobile and American Culture.* Ann Arbor: University of Michigan Press, 1983.

Lowe, Marcia D. *Worldwatch Paper 98: Alternatives to the Automobile.* Washington, DC: The Worldwatch Institute, 1990.

———. *Worldwatch Paper 90: The Bicycle, Vehicle for a Small Planet.* Washington, DC: The Worldwatch Institute, 1989.

Mumford, Lewis. *The Highway and the City.* New York: Mentor, 1963.

Nussbaum, Bruce. *The World After Oil: The Shifting Axis of Power and Wealth.* New York: Simon & Schuster, 1985.

Organization for Economic Cooperation and Development. *The Automobile and the Environment: An International Perspective.* Cambridge, MA: MIT Press, 1978.

Owen, Wilfred. *The Accessible City.* Washington, DC: The Brookings Institution, 1972.

―――. *The Metropolitan Transportation Problem.* Washington, DC: The Brookings Institution, 1966.

Renner, Micael. *Rethinking the Role of the Automobile.* Washington, DC: The Worldwatch Institute, 1988.

Silk, Gerald, et al. *The Automobile and Culture.* New York: Abrams, 1984.

Sperling, Daniel. *New Transportation Fuels.* Berkeley: University of California Press, 1989.

Wark, K., and C. F. Warner. *Air Pollution: Its Origin and Control.* New York: HarperCollins, 1986.

# GLOSSARY

**acid rain**   Precipitation or dry deposition containing sulfuric and nitric acids formed from the burning of fossil fuels.

**assembly line**   An arrangement of laborers, machinery, and equipment in a workplace by which work passes from operation to operation until the product is finished.

**carbon dioxide ($CO_2$)**   A colorless, odorless, incombustible gas released when fossil fuels are burned. Not normally considered an air pollutant, it is among the greenhouse gases that trap heat in the earth's atmosphere, possibly causing global warming.

**carbon monoxide (CO)**   Odorless, invisible toxic gas that is a product of fossil fuel combustion. Its primary source is motor vehicles.

**catalytic converter**   Attachment to an automobile that changes pollutants in exhaust gases into less harmful compounds.

**chlorofluorocarbons (CFCs)**   Gaseous chemical compounds thought to be the primary cause of the degradation of the earth's protective **ozone** layer; used in automobile air-conditioning systems, plastic-foam propellants, and in various other industrial processes.

**ecosystem**   A community of organisms interacting with one another as well as with the physical environment.

**emission standards**   Control strategy requiring specific sources of pollution—such as automobile manufacturers—to install technologies in order to limit emissions.

**greenhouse effect**   The trapping of infrared radiation in the earth's atmosphere by gases such as **carbon dioxide** and methane, resulting in higher temperatures on the earth's surface.

**lead**   A toxic element whose primary atmospheric source is gasoline; can accumulate in the body and eventually damage internal organs.

**nitrogen oxide**   A gas released into the atmosphere by car exhausts, coal, forest fires, and nitrogen-based artificial fertilizers; reacts with other substances in the presence of sunlight to form smog.

**ozone**   The building block of the ozone layer. In the upper layers of the atmosphere, ozone prevents the sun's destructive ultraviolet radiation from reaching the earth's surface. In the lower layers of the atmosphere, it forms as a result of reactions between fossil fuel combustion products and oxygen and can be hazardous to human health.

**particulates**   Air pollutants in the form of solid particles, such as ash, unburned fuels, or metals; or liquid droplets, such as sulfuric or nitric acid. When inhaled, particulates can travel deep into the lungs and cause serious damage.

**petroleum**   A naturally occuring material composed mainly of hydrocarbon compounds. Extracted from underground deposits, it is sent to oil refineries and converted to gasoline, tar, heating oil, and diesel fuel.

**photovoltaic cells**   **Solar energy** devices that convert sunlight directly into electricity.

**ribbon development**   When a town is built consisting of buildings constructed side by side along a highway; causes towns to be strung-out and formless, with no sense of community and no city center.

**solar energy**   Energy produced by converting the sun's heat into electricity or other types of usable energy.

**sulfur dioxide**   A pollutant emitted in fossil fuel combustion that, along with **nitrogen oxides**, is a cause of **acid rain**.

# INDEX

and traffic fatalities, 44–45
and wildlife, 84, 95

Baltimore, Maryland, 53, 65
Bangkok, Thailand, 80
Barnsbury, England, 39–41
Baylor College of Medicine, 82
Beaver Creek, Colorado, 41–42
Beijing, China, 53
Benz, Karl, 14
Bicycles, 70–72
BMW, 27–28, 51, 61
Bombay, India, 14
Boston, Massachusetts, 22, 44, 69
Boston City Council, 22
Boston Transportation Planning
    Review (BTPR), 22
Brookings Institution, 52
Budapest, Hungary, 28
Buick, 17
Bush, George, 20, 47–48, 50, 64

Cadillac, 17
Cairo, Egypt, 31
Cancer, 82–83
Cape Cod, Massachusetts, 71
Carbon, 18
Carbon dioxide, 25, 29, 82
Carbon monoxide, 18, 27, 29
Center for Auto Safety, 52
Centers for Disease Control, 44
Central Park, 69
Chicago, Illinois, 21, 53, 65, 71
China, 69, 70
Chirac, Jacques, 69
Chlorofluorocarbons (CFCs), 26,
    96–97
Chrysler Corporation, 17, 58
Civic Hatchback VX, 50

Clean Air Act, 20–21, 23, 53–54,
    65, 71–72
Congress, U.S., 20
Cugnot, Nicolas, 13

Daihatsu Charade, 50, 63, 96
Daimler-Benz, 61
Daimler, Gottlieb, 14
Dallas, Texas, 70
Darmon, Richard, 20
Delft, Netherlands, 53
Department of Agriculture, U.S., 85
Department of Energy, U.S., 50,
    61
Detroit, Michigan, 16, 63
Dirty air, 25–26, 28
DNA, 82
Dream, the, 61
Durant, William, 15, 17
Duryea, Charles, 15
Duryea, Frank, 15

Eisenhower, Dwight D., 79
Electricity, 14, 17, 54
Elettra, 58
Emission standards, 26
Energy Action, 50
England, 13, 47
Environmental Protection Agency
    (EPA), 20, 29, 92, 93, 96
Environmental Quality
    Improvement Act, 19
European Commission, 58
Exxon Valdez, 31

Federal Aid Highway Act of 1944,
    85–86
Federal Aid Highway Act of 1956,
    86

National Highway Traffic Safety
  Administration, 45
Natural gas, 54
Netherlands, 59, 70
*New England Journal of Medicine,*
  29
New Jersey, 26, 81
New York, 26, 81
New York City, 21, 31, 53, 65, 69,
  73, 74
Nitrogen, 18
*Nitrogen oxide,* 18, 25, 26

Office of Environmental Quality,
  19
Oil spills, 25, 30–31
Oldsmobile, 17
Olds, Ransom Eli, 14, 15
Olds Motor Works, 16
Operation Desert Storm, 47
Orlando, Florida, 63, 81
Osaka, Japan, 58
Otto, Nikolaus August, 14
Owen, Wilfred, 36, 87–88
Oxygen, 18
*Ozone,* 26
Ozone layer, 96

Paris, France, 69
Parliament, British, 13
Pathfinder, 81
Peachtree City, Georgia, 42–43
Pennsylvania Railroad, 44
Persian Gulf, 48, 53
Philadelphia, Pennsylvania, 21,
  44, 53
Phoenix, Arizona, 70
Piedmont Park, 69
Prospect Park, 69
Public Citizen, 52

Randerath, Kurt, 82–83
Ra-Ra, 61
Reagan, Ronald, 23, 64
Renner, Michael, 81–82
Rome, Italy, 80
Russia, 14, 70

Sagan, Carl, 47
San Diego, California, 53, 77
San Francisco, 23
San Francisco Bay Area Rapid
  Transit, 55
Santa Monica, California, 81
Santa Monica Freeway, 81
Sargent, Francis, 22
*Shinkasen,* 77
Sierra Club, 20
South Coast Air Quality
  Management Plan, 65
Stanford University, 63
Stanley, Francis, 14
Stanley, Freelan, 14
Stanley Steamer, 14
Steam tractor, 13
Suffolk County, New York, 96
Sulfuric acid, 32, 95
Sunrunner, 62–63
SUnSUrfer, 63
Sununu, John, 20, 50
Suzuki Motors, 50, 63
Suzuki Swift, 50, 53, 96
Sweden, 68
Switzerland, 41, 58, 68

Texas A & M University Center for
  Electrochemical Systems, 61
Tokyo, Japan, 80, 81
Toyota, 61
Trans-Australian World Solar
  Challenge, 62

(From U.S./English system units to metric system units)

### Length

1 inch = 2.54 centimeters
1 foot = 0.305 meters
1 yard = 0.91 meters
1 statute mile = 1.6 kilometers (km.)

### Area

1 square yard = 0.84 square meters
1 acre = 0.405 hectares
1 square mile = 2.59 square km.

### Liquid Measure

1 fluid ounce = 0.03 liters
1 pint (U.S.) = 0.47 liters
1 quart (U.S.) = 0.95 liters
1 gallon (U.S.) = 3.78 liters

### Weight and Mass

1 ounce = 28.35 grams
1 pound = 0.45 kilograms
1 ton = 0.91 metric tons

### Temperature

1 degree Fahrenheit = 0.56 degrees Celsius or centigrade, but to convert from actual Fahrenheit scale measurements to Celsius, subtract 32 from the Fahrenheit reading, multiply the result by 5, and then divide by 9. For example, to convert 212° F to Celsius:

$212 - 32 = 180 \times 5 = 900 \div 9 = 100°\,C$

## A B O U T   T H E   A U T H O R

MAXINE ROCK is an author and journalist specializing in health and the environment. She is a fellow of the Rackham School of Graduate Studies in Journalism of the University of Michigan and a fellow of the Knight Center for Specialized Journalism at the University of Maryland. Her articles have appeared in national and international magazines, and she is the author of four books. Rock is a founding member of the Atlanta Coalition on the Transportation Crisis, vice-president of the PATH Foundation, and has served on the Mayor's Transportation Committee for Atlanta. She is also a member of the American Society of Journalists and Authors.

## A B O U T   T H E   E D I T O R

RUSSELL E. TRAIN, currently chairman of the board of directors of the World Wildlife Fund and The Conservation Foundation, has had a long and distinguished career of government service under three presidents. In 1957 President Eisenhower appointed him a judge of the United States Tax Court. He served Lyndon Johnson on the National Water Commission. Under Richard Nixon he became under secretary of the Interior and, in 1970, first chairman of the Council on Environmental Quality. From 1973 to 1977 he served as administrator of the Environmental Protection Agency. Train is also a trustee or director of the African Wildlife Foundation; the Alliance to Save Energy; the American Conservation Association; Citizens for Ocean Law; Clean Sites, Inc.; the Elizabeth Haub Foundation; the King Mahendra Trust for Nature Conservation (Nepal); Resources for the Future; the Rockefeller Brothers Fund; the Scientists' Institute for Public Information; the World Resources Institute; and Union Carbide and Applied Energy Services, Inc. Train is a graduate of Princeton and Columbia Universities, a veteran of World War II, and currently resides in the District of Columbia.